Slightly Foxed
by my theatrical family

SLIGHTLY FOXED
by my theatrical family

Angela Fox

Fontana/Collins

First published in Great Britain by
William Collins Sons & Co. Ltd 1986
First issued in Fontana Paperbacks 1987

Printed and bound in Great Britain by
William Collins Sons & Co. Ltd, Glasgow

Contents

Acknowledgements

I would like to thank Garry O'Connor, my Editor, for his patience, informed criticism and advice during the writing of this book. I have admired his books, but never thought I would have the immense pleasure of actually working with him. I am extremely grateful for all he has done, and the fact that we have become friends is an added bonus.

I would also like to thank Annie Hirst for her endurance in the preparation of the manuscript, keeping one up to the mark, and the fun she brought to the job.

A.F.
Cuckfield, 25.10.85

PART ONE

1

The Doctor's Little Girls

Gentle Jesus, meek and mild,
  Look upon a little child;
Pity my simplicity,
  Suffer me to come to thee.

Life, for the four Worthington daughters, was lived entirely in the nursery. This prayer was said on our knees at the end of every day. I can remember giving it a great deal of thought, repeating it over and over again once I was in bed. The word simplicity pleased me very much; it had a reassuring sound.

Outward conventions were closely observed, but the nursery on the top floor of The Sycamores, Birchington, Kent was a battleground for conflict caused by the grown-ups breaking society's rules. We little girls were the cannon fodder. Elizabeth, born in 1908, was the eldest by four and a half years. She was the daughter of the master of the house, Dr Worthington. The rest of us were illegitimate, a very terrible state of affairs in those days. The rest were Angela – myself, that is – Felicity and Yvonne. We were all beautifully clothed, always well fed. As far as the eye could see we children had everything. But, as the eldest bastard, I felt I knew from the very beginning that nowhere in our house was there very much simplicity.

Dr Worthington was a saint. A tall stooping figure, we would sometimes call Harry, sometimes Daddy. He made no distinction between his own daughter and his wife's love children: for us he was always the father figure. But he could never have been very attractive to my mother, even when she bore Elizabeth. Perhaps she never wanted that. Christened Lucy Glitters and known as Glitters, she was thirty years younger than Harry, and he remained something of a father to her, even when she was being unfaithful to him. Her own father, Charles Morice, had been a rich stockbroker, successful and respected in business and in sport. Her mother was the illegitimate daughter of a coachman, spotted when Morice was shooting with friends in Derbyshire. She died when Glitters was three.

Charles Morice rented a house in Birchington during the summer when his yacht was at Ramsgate. Harry and Glitters met when she fell ill with measles. Harry was not only respected and loved as the village doctor, he was famous for the use of his hands – finding a tumour, diagnosing an appendix. He saw you into life, and he saw you through death. What's more, he cared. He was nothing if not steady and he loved Glitters all his life, and she was totally dependent on him. On one occasion she tried to tell him: 'I'm going to leave you, because I don't love you.' But he replied: 'You're going to stay with me because I do love you.'

It was a very buttoned-up age, that of the First World War and its aftermath. It put stresses and strains on young women, especially young married women, unheard of today. Glitters had quickly become the doctor's pretty little wife, and was indeed very pretty. But Harry, apart from his age, and two slightly deformed feet, had a further disability.

'Poor Harry's impotent, you know,' she shocked us one day by declaring. 'He can't do it – Thank God!' she added.

But this confession came later.

Her life, in the early years of their marriage, was wrapped in secrecy. She needed men physically; for a woman of her class, that was something to be deeply ashamed of. And affairs could be very messy, especially in a small, tight community like Birchington. Hence Glitters' black moods when she entered our nursery, which we were only allowed to leave when Nanny permitted. Mummy was not going to have small children 'rampaging around the house'. Even then, I knew this was because she 'entertained' in her pretty bedroom on the floor below. Many of these visitors were ladies and there was much sound of gossip and laughter. But the most frequent visitor of all was called Mr Lonsdale.

Frederick Leonard Lonsdale, born in 1881 and aged thirty-one when I, his first love child, came into the world, was a famous playwright of light, social comedies like *On Approval* and *Aren't We All?* For a writer he was odd: he read little, had a poor opinion of Shakespeare, and never kept a dictionary in the house. His best known play was *The Last of Mrs Cheyney*, though this, being a crime thriller, was not a typical work. At one time five plays of his were running in the West End: his marvellously brittle and sophisticated style tempted the greatest acting names of his day like Gerald du Maurier, Charles Hawtrey, Yvonne Arnaud and Gladys Cooper.

The penniless and self-educated son of a Jersey tobacconist, Lonsdale was a fascinating man, with wonderful hair and a distinctive style of dressing. (My son Edward later adopted his grandfather's habit, which he had neither seen nor heard about, of always wearing white socks and a white scarf – wool for daytime, silk for night.) Freddy married an artillery colonel's daughter, Leslie Hoggan, and for many years the struggle was hard. When starting out, still poor and unknown, he wrote the librettos for a number of operettas including *The Maid of the Mountains, Madame Pompadour* and *Monsieur Beaucaire*. With Leslie at his side, Freddy began the long social climb to his daily ration of champagne, which in later life he used to decant into a jug, and to his acceptance in the very highest circles as a celebrity.

Although he remained married to Leslie all his life and was, from the accounts of his three legitimate daughters, a devoted if eccentric father, Freddy was impatient and distrustful by nature and tended to play off people against one another, perhaps to cover his tremendous fear of deep emotional ties. But he would get drawn in nevertheless, as he did in his affair with Glitters.

As far as I can piece it together, this began when he made a pass at Kitty Richardson, otherwise Mrs Alfred Douglas-Hamilton, a bored but highly clever society beauty who declined his advances but suggested that he might 'Go and amuse the little sister', this being Glitters, her illegitimate half-sister. The Lonsdales had moved to Westgate-on-Sea, near Birchington, and opportunities for their meeting were frequent; as the doctor's wife, Glitters would call on Harry's patients, and Harry and Glitters and Leslie and Freddy soon became firm friends.

When Freddy came to the house he would whistle for my mother, and when he talked to me and my sisters he would speak to us as adults, entertaining us hugely with stories of his minor or even imaginary complaints which he was convinced would be fatal – we found it funny that he could take them so seriously.

Glitters, who was a great reader, would make out to us that Freddy's success was a matter of luck, that he was feckless, that he had no technique, but this was not true at all. His plays have stood the test of time and only recently *Aren't We All* had a record-breaking run at the Haymarket Theatre, with Rex Harrison and Claudette Colbert. But at the time I did not know their qualities and believed her. Freddy based all his plots on observation of class and manners, on the way he played with people, and he delighted in the ironies of any situation: cuckolding dear Harry, for example, while at the same time placing his life, when he was ill, in Harry's hands. In *Canaries Sometimes Sing*, when Geoffrey Lymes, a successful light playwright, exclaims in mock consternation: 'My home broken asunder, and by my best friend! For a playwright, how little I know of life,' his levity was just like Freddy's.

But the seriousness of the affair was registered in a very different way in my mother's days of black rage. On one occasion I must have been making some tiresome noise in our nursery. This more often than not exceedingly charming and amusing woman appeared at the door in her dressing-gown, seized me violently and, pushing me ahead of her, hit me repeatedly on the head. I fell down the stairs to the landing, finally hurting myself quite badly, on an oak chest on which she had carefully arranged her willow pattern china. Another time I was punished for some misdemeanour by being dragged and lumped into a hideous horsehair sofa, the most revoltingly uncomfortable piece of furniture in the nursery. My face was pressed to the wall – the sofa was turned round – and I cannot even remember trying to get out over the side with its carved mahogany top.

The blackest day of all was when Nanny was sacked. Nanny Bowler was God-fearing, goody-goody, wispy and delicate. She was Chapel – Wesleyan. We thought that hugely funny. There were pictures in the nursery of Jesus Christ as a droopy, rather colourless man, draped in a white sheet, clutching a lamb. He had a sickly-sweet expression and a halo. Nanny taught us he was our total boss.

During the summers Nanny often took us swimming. She would pack my two younger sisters into the pram along with buckets and spades, towels, bathing costumes, warm clothes to change into and Petit Beurre biscuits, and we set out for Minnis Bay and the beach. We walked fast and in silence. Nanny seemed full of inner crossness. She had too much to do in the nursery and this idea of Dr Worthington's that the girls must swim was a lot of nonsense. However, Nanny obeyed orders: Dr Worthington – she always referred to him that way – gave very few orders but when he did he was obeyed. She carried out our mother's orders, too, but we were well aware that she disapproved of most of them.

One day when I was about seven, on the staircase between the nursery and the landing Nanny Bowler and my mother had a blazing row over my mother's continuing infidelities and Nanny was told once and for all to get out. That black day was also a day of growing up, of being aware for the first time of other people's misery, and for the first time of feeling affection for Nanny, even gratitude, compassion, if you like. I decided in that moment that I, too, would get out, but voluntarily, and as soon as I could. I felt impotent fury towards my mother, and throughout my childhood, that never quite left me.

During those early years, by way of compensation for the terrors and complications of the adult world, I lived a vivid fantasy life in which I became 'Mrs Jones'. 'Mrs Jones' was a busy, energetic woman with far, far too much to do. Her husband, Captain Jones, was away at the war shooting Germans with a sharp stick, and he expected her to do everything, but everything. She did not like him much, but he was her Better Half. She had not actually seen him for a very long time because he never got leave, but she could describe him most graphically. Captain Jones was short, strong, dark and violent and always on the go. He had a trim black moustache and he never took his cap off. He was very, very smart, and carried a cane under his arm. He was always barking commands and, because he did not get leave, he wrote a great many letters about how he was Winning the War, and so banished all fear on that score from Mrs Jones's life. He never came home – just as well, because he was obviously a humourless bore. Nonetheless, Mrs Jones sometimes felt she would like to make the journey to see him, and would mount the nursery rocking horse and ride for hours and hours towards The Front where he was waiting for her. The journey never tired her, and she never arrived, which was a very good thing because it meant that she must set out again on this wonderful journey early the next day.

I am not sure why Mrs Jones was always so very busy, for she had only one child. He was Peter, her adored son, a wax doll very plain with one arm, who was always stark naked. No son ever had more love than Mrs Jones felt for him, but she was useless at dressing him, having no gifts at all in that direction. He had her love to keep him warm.

My mother, when she was playing the doctor's wife, did all the right things. She was so captivating and so interested in all his patients that she made a great success in the role. She longed to be part of Freddy's group. The Lonsdales and their neighbours, the actor Gerald du Maurier and his wife Muriel with their three daughters, and Gladys Cooper, her husband, Herbert Buckmaster, founder of the famous Buck's Club, with their children, Joan and John, all used their houses in Kent. My mother was stage-struck, dazzled by them, but apart from being Freddy's lady love on the side – and they were quite nice to her – she never really became a member of their circle. Her endless talk of 'Gerald' and 'Gladys' and all their theatrical friends never rang quite true; even more did I feel an outsider.

Standing in the wings watching the group of theatrical celebrities gathered at Birchington for their children's summer holidays, one person stood out to me who seemed quite perfect, and that was Gladys Cooper. Gladys was a great star – these were days when television did not exist – famous for her beauty and her clothes as much as for her acting.

She had taken a house in Birchington because Gerald du Maurier, with whom she was starring in *The Last of Mrs Cheyney* at London's St James's Theatre, had a house there, and because Freddy had taken one nearby.

Some years before this period, when Joan and John were very small, she had taken a house at Frinton and had met there a family called Fox. They had three children then and the two older ones, Mary and Kenneth, played on the beach with her two. There was also a fat baby in a pram; he was called Robin. Robin's mother, Hilda, was totally obsessed by the beauty of this fat baby. Gladys, rather irritated by the over-maternal carry-on of the Jewish Momma act, one day took the baby from the pram and ran off with him, and hid just long enough to hear the hysterical screams when the empty pram was discovered. Gladys loved to tell this story when the years had passed and the Fat Baby had become her closest confidant and manager.

Now, every evening when the curtain came down, Gladys and Gerald would get in a car and drive to Birchington so that the days could be spent with the children, and in the mid-afternoon they set out for London again. Then and always Gladys's passion in life was children, her own particularly, but anyone's children drew her like a magnet. Gladys playing cricket with the Birchington children on the beach, Gladys swimming, Gladys doling out the picnic lunch: the picture I have of her is like a sunburned, athletic boy, with golden curly hair – the astonishing beauty of the face, particularly the eyes, took over when she was dressed and ready to leave for London. When she had gone it really was as if the light had gone out; she may not have been a great actress – although she became better and better with the years – but she was a great woman, and a leader; everyone had to do their best, be their best, for Gladys.

I remember Daphne du Maurier as a small girl as if she were in my garden now, with her wonderful blonde hair and a straight, slim body. She invariably dressed in emerald green stockinet pullover and shorts but never played with the rest of us: always, when I recall her, she is lying face down in some long grass, reading, never talking, never joining in, always reading. Her sisters, Angela and Jeanne, were fairly friendly to me.

Contact with Quex Park, the 'Big House' in Birchington, was a fixed part of childhood. Quex Park was owned by the Powell-Cottons. Major Powell-Cotton had an amazing museum full of wild animals he had shot and stuffed: elephants, lions, tigers, hippos, crocodiles, giraffes – nothing had been spared. The Major had a beard and we hardly ever saw more of him than a glimpse, a detached smile: I would pretend to myself that he was Secret Service. The house was enormous and very polished, and there was a frightening room called 'The Library'. We saw this occasionally and were always glad to get out. The garden was very fine, great lawns and big fir trees, but very impersonal. There were swings, but they appeared not to want you to swing on them.

The Major had a huge, beautiful, patronizing wife called Hannah and I wished he had shot and stuffed her too. It was at Quex Park that I learned who my father was. It was a perfect summer's day. We were picnicking in a meadow and I had wandered a short way from the gossiping nannies. In the long, dry grass and among the wild marguerites where very small blue butterflies had a hectically busy time, I had departed to paradise.

Here I could indulge in my passionate summer job, that of catching defenceless – but very wily – grasshoppers and placing them captive in a cardboard shoe box.

The Powell-Cotton nanny was a virago called Cooker. Cooker's voice droned on and on. I was hardly listening. It was of no interest to me. But I have little doubt that naughty old Cooker raised her voice deliberately: 'Well, of course, she's difficult, isn't she, illegitimate and all that? Mr Lonsdale, her father, doesn't even work! Poor Dr Worthington is what we all say.'

We were a great deal at Quex Park because Hannah worshipped Dr Worthington. Hannah's attitude to the Doctor's children was that she supposed she must do her best for those poor little unwanted things – 'in one's position one must do one's best, mustn't one?'

How did my sisters respond to their extraordinary early life? Elizabeth, Harry's legitimate daughter, was a loner, sent to a rotten boarding school which she loathed. Love child number two was Felicity, three years my junior, round and bonny, nicknamed Nutkin to this day. The third love child was Yvonne. She was born when love had grown very thin and Freddy was ready for full flight to London where the applause was ringing and where Amazonian ladies with titles and backgrounds waited. Of Yvonne I remember very little. She was seven years younger than me and we are strangers to this day, polite and well-behaved, but strangers. I recall enormous, very pale, rather beautiful blue eyes – sad, but the bluest I have ever seen.

My sisters and I were perfectly aware of Hannah's attitude and for me it was an accepted shadow in our relationship with the members of her household. We were different and thus not quite right. I was puzzled and depressed by the labels grown-ups gave children. Nothing I did ever just happened, it was because I was illegitimate, I was evilly motivated, I was bad. However, I also found out that I could be termed 'That very plain but amusing child', and I learned many tricks that made life a little easier.

I do not know whether it was that overheard nursery gossip which caused me to become, in the months that followed, an intensely difficult, hysterical creature, but something did. I do know that I caused real depression and misery for those around me, particularly for my mother and Harry, who was now in the early stages of Parkinson's disease and beginning to grow enfeebled. In only a little while I became a panic-stricken child dominated by some agonizing fear which was not understood and never diagnosed. The ever-recurring sentence with which I was admonished – 'Stop trying to call attention to yourself!' – was a waste of breath. Perhaps this is what I was desperately trying to do. If so I paid a hideous price for my efforts in attacks of hysteria that came on every evening.

A sense of panic would overtake me and as if to ward it off, I deliberately started to breathe deeply, violently, and to scream and shout. This performance affected everyone unhappily – everyone, that is, except for Freddy who was not even faintly interested. My sisters hated it – and me; I can't blame them. I would moan and gasp and scream for hours, until physical fatigue would produce a sudden calm, and rather good sleep. Then I would wake up refreshed and quite normal, while the rest of the household was worn out. They would taunt and tease me about 'Having the feeling', which became the accepted name for my fits of misery. How stupid I was, they told me, how undisciplined, and worse, how 'potty' – the family term for insane. But it was no joke for anyone. The words that dominated those fraught attacks of mine were 'Fetch Daddy, fetch Daddy – I'm dying, I'm dying.' I remember vividly how it was Dr Worthington I wanted, and how I wished violently that I was not just dying but DEAD. Dying meant to be consumed by Fear, to be dead was to be released. I also remember that if Dr Worthington did appear, which he sometimes did, he could calm me almost at once. My mother resented this skill of his and would shout, 'Leave her alone, Harry, that's just what she wants – to call attention to herself.' I think he understood the situation very well. The reason he did not make more effort to stand up to my mother was that he was getting steadily more ill and tired himself.

But I did go from Hell to Heaven, sometimes. Heaven was to be taken by Dr Worthington in his Renault to a village about five miles away called Sarre to stay with 'The Champs'. They were a childless couple called Maud and Sydney Champion, and they lived in a white farmhouse called The Elms. Maud was the fattest woman I have ever known, with white 'bobbed' hair, well cut and cared for. She wore country clothes of tweed and cashmere, choosing them in good colours, pale greens and mauves, and had expensive shoes.

A calm, smiling, amiable woman, Maud teased me in a laughing, good-natured way and when I went to my room at night she would tell me, 'You won't get "the feeling" while you're staying here, but if you ever feel it coming on at all, what you have to do is to come and tell me, and it will go away.' So 'the feeling' never had to be thought of, let alone talked about, at The Elms. Sydney would take me round his farm, and he would let me feed the chickens. We watched the milking of the cows, performed by dairy maids in those days, and Sydney would hold my hand. The calm comfort and joy that both he and Maud gave me will live with me always.

The high spot of the Champs's year was Canterbury Cricket Week. A fabulous picnic of hams and pies and huge sponge cakes made by Maud would be packed into the hamper, and off to the Cricket Ground we would motor. The weather of course was quite perfect, and there can never have been grander trees than there were at the Canterbury Cricket Ground. The only sound was of the ball against the bat. Best of all, I fell in love with a member of my team, Kent. His name was Frank Woolley. I queued up with masses of other children to get his autograph and naturally I was the only one Frank Woolley was even faintly interested in, I was confident of that.

Dr Worthington also arranged our annual holiday, and here again 'the feeling' hardly ever put in an appearance. The holiday was at Ditchling in Sussex, about eighty miles away, but had it been as far as Australia it could not have been more of an adventure. Our mother usually came too and she was at her best – calm and enjoying herself. On these holidays she had her friend, a successful novelist called Parry Truscott: they would talk away the days sitting on the South Downs. We would walk to these from the village and climb Ditchling Beacon.

*

I was sent to various schools, and failed, and failed, and failed again. I did not believe I could do my lessons – in my eyes I was a mistake, an accident, a mess. But I did learn very early on to get other people to do the work for me, and that what I had to do in return was to amuse them. This was my forte. Above all I wanted to be popular, to be liked and loved.

At home I was not loved. Love takes time and there was too little of that. I felt I was a nuisance and an embarrassment. At school I giggled a lot and told marvellous lies. I entered a world of fantasy. I was the girl who knew all, *all* the famous stars of the theatre. But a schoolgirl stuffing everyone's autograph book with fake signatures was a menace and, to teachers, a headache. I did not work and caused my classmates to giggle and gossip.

So it was a great day for Miss Russell, one of my headmistresses, when she found reason to expel me. My desire to be popular made me think it a lark to take notes from the girls I longed to impress and give them to boys cramming for Oxford and Cambridge, whose digs I had to pass on my way home. I was caught, and found myself in Miss Russell's study. She was Austrian, a great snob and an ardent Roman Catholic. She thought herself a great success with her school – but I had failed her. Her lips compressed with anger, she spoke in a crescendo: 'You are a bad girl. You are a wicked girl. You are evil. There is no hope. I have prayed ceaselessly for you, I have lit a candle for you every day. But you are NO GOOD. YOU NEVER WILL BE.'

Drawing herself together with a shudder she told me to leave then and there, and good riddance.

I learned what anguish meant. My mother thought 'Miss Russie' was right, and didn't know what the hell she was going to do with me. She seriously contemplated mental homes, and let me know it. Fortunately my half-sister, Frances, had been a great success at a school called Bromley Old Palace: she'd never put a foot wrong. The headmistress there, Miss Millicent MacTaggart, had retired but retirement had not suited her, and when she heard of a Dr and Mrs Box who wanted to start a small school for difficult girls near Stratford-upon-Avon, she went into partnership with them as head of the teaching side. My mother heard of this school through Leslie Lonsdale and thought, 'If Frances can be such a success, this Miss MacTaggart might do better than some with Angela.'

This was how we came to be, one fine day, in her study at Avoncliffe. My first going-over was with Miss MacTaggart herself. She was a tall, brawny Scotswoman, fading red hair dragged back from her face into a bun. Her clothes were nondescript green and beige, her hands strong and masculine, but it is always the eyes I remember of every human being I have ever met. 'Tag's' were not beautiful, they were pale green and past their prime, but they looked at you, they took you in and you communicated with her through them. She knew at once that this liar before her was very truthful. She also told me that day that she was going to enjoy teaching me, because I was intelligent. This amazed me, but I have been intelligent since that moment. That moment when I was accepted at Avoncliffe, I took on the world.

I fell in love, for the first time, with a house. The white, two-storeyed building, which later became the home of Peter Hall and Leslie Caron, was right on the river and the water lapped the walls. Childhood memories are nearly always of summer, and I recall strenuous tennis in the afternoons on the slightly neglected grass court. Then, sitting on the steps of the rock garden that led to the water, we used to watch the lazy river traffic until dusk fell. We rarely saw motor boats, and when we did they were very small; punts, elegantly handled, and rowing boats were the craft of the river then. Strains of music would occasionally drift towards us from a wind-up gramophone – that was real happiness for a group of tired girls who, until now, had been unmanageable.

Tag knew I would never be with her long – the fees would only be paid occasionally and we had a sort of silent, even grown-up understanding about this. She told me we would work together on *Hamlet* and on the essays of Hazlitt, and this is exactly what she stuck to. For the first time in my life I learned the pleasure of working and concentrating, and of reading alone – no longer needing to create an effect on others.

The old theatre at Stratford had been burned down, the present one not yet built. A first-rate company played at the local cinema, though, and we went to the theatre every single week of the season. This became a basic part of my education and confirmed my passion for the theatre. I never wanted anything except to be an actress. Tag accepted this. And so at sixteen I left her, having at least learned a few fragments of English literature.

*

Freddy had disappeared from our lives just before adolescence overtook me. After about fourteen years he had grown tired of my mother, and he and Lesley now spent more time together – and apart – in London. Among his patrons were now the Londonderrys, the Dudley-Wards, even the Prince of Wales. Freddy's eye had been caught by Lady Maureen Stanley, Lord Londonderry's sister, who was the wife of Oliver Stanley, a member of the cabinet. But the problem was, how could he ditch Glitters? The materials for an explosion that might achieve this were always to hand, but who could provide the fuse – and light it?

The answer lay in a widow, a gossipy go-between named Nini

Albertson. Freddy wickedly told Nini that Glitters had seduced him a long time ago, but now the affair was going badly and he wanted to end it. Nini, set alight with a sense of outrage, went to Leslie, who of course had known of the liaison for years. Nini supplied Leslie with the opportunity to feign total surprise and great anguish at the sudden discovery of this dreadful, illicit relationship. She stormed along to Glitters. The upshot was that provided my mother and my father never met again, my father would guarantee that Miss Cheshire, his secretary, would send my mother £100 a year for each illegitimate daughter.

The offer was accepted. From that moment forth my mother cancelled out love from her life. She taught us that men have no feelings whatever and that they never, never, never speak the truth about anything. She taught us that men are totally and utterly unreliable (unless they are good and unattractive like Harry, and that does not count). The man she loved had proved a bastard, and didn't give a damn about the Love Children. He didn't, either. I have never had a kiss from a mother or father.

As Freddy's star continued to rise, so did Harry's go more and more downhill. He tried to keep his practice going but his condition now deteriorated drastically and one day, after Freddy had left Glitters, he was called in to treat his nine-year-old niece, Ruth, who had a pain in her stomach. He palpated her carefully with his famous hands, but mistakenly pronounced that she had not got appendicitis. A few days later, in terrible agony, she died. Harry was so stricken with remorse that he disappeared. They found him, after dark, in a haystack, trying to hide. He was crying bitterly.

As a doctor, Harry was finished. He tried sharing the practice with a small man with a dark moustache called Dr Andrews but it had been mismanaged for years, and Dr Andrews took to the bottle and then fled. Finally it was sold to a youngish, stout, blond bounder called Hayes. My mother put Harry into the care of Nurse White, a huge woman in a pleated white bonnet, settling him in a tiny cottage on the Powell-Cotton estate. As for herself

– and for us – Glitters had decided where the future lay. She took a maisonette in London at 16a Lower Belgrave Street, above a cake shop.

'I must make a good address for the girls,' she said.

2

Lower Belgrave Street

When Glitters found her good address for the girls we were ready to fly the nest, but not too far, so that it suited us all very well. For the year or two before, Nutkin and Yvonne were mostly at school and were sent to stay with friends rather too often in the holidays. I had already got into the Royal Academy of Dramatic Art, and had for a short time till the family move been living on the top floor of a boarding house in Primrose Hill. How I scraped into RADA will always be a mystery to me: I was too fat, rather plain, and the authorities knew my fees would never get paid; far worse, so did I.

Glitters had hardly a penny in the world and must, most days, have been an intensely worried woman. We left all the work, all the responsibility of the move to her. This was, however, quite what she expected and accepted. Her attitude to challenge was typified by the American song 'Pick yourself up, dust yourself off and start all over again'.

She had to find the rent for our good address, which was around five pounds a week. Harry must be kept at the cottage and before anything else, Nurse White's wages must be paid. Then she was generous to a fault and tried to see that we had everything we needed. Had it been possible she would probably have spoiled us. Her father had named her Lucy Glitters after the horse on which he had had a good win on the day of her birth, and she had inherited his instinct for backing a hunch.

Lower Belgrave Street was her gamble to help her daughters achieve what she believed to be their rightful position in life. In private she would still yell and scream and lambast us for being lazy, irresponsible and ill-mannered, which we took in good part, knowing she was right but going our own way. We accepted her public performance equally carelessly, but she exercised great charm and had a great sense of humour and a really inspiring sense of the enjoyment of day-to-day living, no matter what the problems were. She believed in creating a background from which four ladies would emerge and conquer the world. She had absolutely no knowledge of the French language but every day we would hear her say at some time or another, 'Je managerai.' This was her watchword, and she reassured herself with it over and over again.

Before we arrived at our good address suitable families, particularly favoured if they were vaguely connected with the aristocracy, had been found for Elizabeth to go to where she could earn a few shillings a week as a sort of au pair. She sewed beautifully and was 'good with the dogs'. One could almost hear her hosts – her employers – remarking: 'No money, you know, but I think you could almost say the mother was a lady'.

Elizabeth was the exact opposite of a career woman; she disliked the social scene and must have been very unhappy, but she never said so. Like her father, Harry, she never expressed herself easily, but she had, even when young, stoicism and dignity. After we had settled in London she began learning to paint furniture in Soho.

Her employers were the Thornton Smiths, who at that time owned Fortnum and Mason. She earned very little here too and must have felt a long way from bringing her own, and part of Glitters', dream true. Marriage, a home of her own and as many dogs as possible, were Elizabeth's ambitions. Her strength has always been in knowing exactly what she wanted. She had a very clear picture of herself as a rather well-bred, English countrywoman. She was practical, a good cook and needle-woman, and from Harry inherited two hobbies she really enjoyed, painting and gardening. It would not be fair to say she didn't want to work; in fact she did work – and still works – harder than anybody I know, but only on things she wanted to do, which at that moment suited her to do. She was very 'throw away the ladder, I'm on board'.

I'm not sure whether my mother liked her – I'm not certain she liked any of us – but Elizabeth was the one she did spoil. She gave in to her every whim and one of these was Elizabeth's conviction, when we were at Lower Belgrave Street, that a woman of breeding could not possibly remain in London once 'the Season' was over. The end of the Season for us consisted of reading in the *Tatler* – when we could afford a copy – that Ascot was over, Henley was under way and that those who mattered were moving towards Goodwood and finally Cowes, before packing up to leave for Scotland and the Glorious Twelfth. I admit Elizabeth knew these dizzy heights were not for her – at least not until she made her dream come true – but she succeeded in brow-beating her mother into scraping up the money to buy a second-hand car in which to set off for a cottage in the country that Glitters had fooled someone into letting her have for her girls' summer holiday.

At any season food in our house was adequate, but unless there was a dinner party for some admirer considered suitable, there was never any drink. We talked about our lack of money every day. It was a nagging worry at the back of everything but somehow I cannot remember that it ever stopped any of us doing exactly what we wanted, and I am glad to have learned to make little, sometimes nothing, go a long way. In fact Glitters loved a gin and tonic and the effect of one would, within moments, make her garrulous, even hilarious. Another favourite expression of hers on days when things went right was 'Everything is the colour of the rose.'

Before we had left Birchington, when Harry could no longer walk, only shuffle, and after Freddy, Glitters had taken a lover. He was commander of the local RAF Manston. I had loathed him. There was no deep, psychological reason for this. It was simply that he could not stand me and I did so much want to be loved by any Tom, Dick or Harry. I became very difficult when this was not the case. We had no servants any more and Glitters did all the work very badly and hated it. But when the Wing Commander had come to stay, she used to dress up like a pretty stage maid and kept carrying trays daintily laid for him, with much show of how heavy these trays were. I was nauseated but the Freddy side of me laughed till I cried and I made my friends laugh by mimicking my mother. 'Go on, Angela, tell us again.' How cruel the young can be.

*

Soon after she arrived in London, Glitters and I developed a passion for going to the theatre. I have no idea where we found the money, although only a small amount was needed, at the most a few shillings. We either sat in the pit, which today is the back of the stalls and which cost 3/6d., or in the gallery for less than two shillings. From Lower Belgrave Street, by walking into Grosvenor Gardens we could catch a bus to Shaftesbury Avenue. The journey cost 2d. After the show we nearly always walked home along Piccadilly, discussing every detail of the perform- ance. The theatre made a lasting impression on me. Many of the plays were not great but they provided wonderful entertainment. I was much more critical and hard to please than Glitters, and if we disagreed at all it was because she had adored every moment.

The mirror Shakespeare wrote about was held up to nature by very fine actors in those pre-Second World War years. They interpreted writers such as Somerset Maugham, Frederick Lonsdale, Nöel Coward and sometimes revivals of Bernard Shaw. These writers demanded a lot of work and very high standards from their actors. It was not such a director-dominated theatre as today, though some names loomed very large, particu- larly that of Basil Dean, whose production of *The Constant Nymph* I shall never forget. The new young actor, John Gielgud, secured in this contemporary play one of his earliest triumphs away from the classics. His performance is as clear to me now as if I had seen it yesterday. The morning after I did see it I got Elizabeth to cut my hair in the same way as Edna Best, the touching vulnerable nymph. I did look silly: Edna Best was fair and frail and very slight; I was fair and strong, giggly and rather fat. But I *felt* just like her and I acted the part very seriously all to myself when no one was looking. I saved up and went to this play quite often; later on in the run John Gielgud took over from Nöel Coward.

Another time I remember an American actress called Jane Cowl in Coward's *Easy Virtue*. She wore a marvellous red dress and when, in the play, the whole of life became too much for her she smashed a very large and immensely valuable vase to the ground. Down came the curtain. Glitters and I strolled home through the Mall discussing how often we felt this need to smash things up. We would look up at the trees; the lamps seemed to have been planted into them.

We would stroll past Hatchards the bookshop and she would repeat to me the agonizing scandal of Clarence Hatry, whom she had once met. Hatry was a city speculator whose enterprises had crashed and who, in a sensational trial for fraud, had been sent to Maidstone Jail, where he became a model prisoner. When released, Hatry had bought Hatchards. We always had the same conversation about him:

Glitters: He was a very attractive man.
Me: Oh, Mummy, how can he have been? He was so ugly.
Glitters: Men are always attractive if they are powerful. And a man who is powerful and kind as well – he is irresistible.

As we strolled, I thought about this a good deal. Men were very important to us both. We could never manage without them and we did not intend to try.

Glitters would sometimes continue, 'You must learn about life. See that girl over there – beautifully dressed, well made up . . . high heels. She's a prostitute.'

I would remonstrate, 'Ah but, Mummy, prostitutes . . .'

She would never let me finish. 'They're usually very nice women who do a good job. They provide a jolly nice evening. They cheer men up. Men are so repressed all the time, and their lives so terribly dull. The girls are a tonic.'

'Look,' I'd say. 'There's another one over there.'

'Oh,' my mother would say in an exasperated tone, 'you are so unobservant. There's nothing in that girl that resembles a prostitute. She is a pretty, hardworking secretary, waiting for the bus to take her home and she's probably terrified that a man will accost her. You must try to tell the difference between people.'

I enjoyed these evenings with my mother and if the weather was fine when we left the theatre I would say, 'Oh do let's walk and we will do our prostitute/secretary chat.' Glitters could be very good company when she escaped the stresses of life for short periods and I have always thought that for her, indeed for a great many people, that is why the theatre is so important.

*

Though I loved the theatre, RADA and I were never really in harmony. I made some good friends, though – conventional hard workers are often devoted to rebels. I would sit in the canteen for hours, watching the comings and goings, gossiping with my chosen few, while any money I had went on tea and doughnuts. My figure was not good anyway and my complexion remained pale and pasty.

The teacher who appealed most to me was Alice Gachet, who was French and had authority and style, though sadly I was neither good enough nor serious enough to be taught by her. I did, however, find myself passionately interested in the potential of other students, among them Peggy Ashcroft, who, although at the Central School was often a visitor at RADA, Celia Johnson, and Charles Laughton.

Peggy seemed clear-headed, down-to-earth, tough and sure of herself; I say 'seemed' only because I wasn't close to her. Celia was so pretty, vulnerable, almost ethereal; the tilt of her head, the touching, apprehensive eyes made the fat girl student Angela Worthington wish she could do something for her, but of course that was impossible. Celia was already outstanding and her career was soon under way, playing in *Cynara* with Gladys Cooper and Gerald du Maurier.

From the very start Charles Laughton was recognizably a genius. I can see him now, sweeping into the RADA Common Room with his coat cloak-wise over his shoulders, heading straight for the food counter. It must be that they had a hidden store of myrrh and incense for the fabulous, booming, spluttering giant, that at the very least the Dom Perignon was on ice. But no – with passion and towering majesty he commanded a Cadbury's milk chocolate bar, and a small one at that.

I decided after only a short while at RADA that I needed to get a job. I wasn't doing any proper work there and the vexed question of fees kept recurring. In those days there were plenty of touring companies which went round what were called either Number one dates or Number two dates, and these offered the best opportunity of work. I sat nervously in the waiting rooms of many theatrical agents and touring managers, thinking nevertheless that I would never be lucky enough. One day I found myself in the office of a beady manager in pince-nez called Lionel Bute. He engaged me immediately, without even an audition, to go on tour in a play called *Just Married* by H. F. Maltby. Mr Maltby was not consulted; I was told to present myself for rehearsal at once. Someone must have let them down. I spent my seventeenth birthday on a Sunday train to Glasgow.

On Monday we opened. I was a professional actress. I received £3.10.0d a week, I had no direction at all, other than a bit of shouting from Mr Maltby, and in two or three weeks I learned more than RADA could ever teach. That tour was true work, and it gave no time for messing about. I was in any case too new and too nervous to get up to any tiresome tricks, but playing in three different towns to people of varied temperaments and interests was a challenge and I loved it.

Since Freddy Lonsdale had disappeared from our lives we

had kept up with him through newspapers for now, as a famous playwright, he continued to enjoy successes both in London and New York. After this tour of mine the fact of my existence was forced on him, I believe through Leslie. Anyway, Freddy said that I could go and see him.

I waited in nervous anguish for what seemed like many lifetimes in the foyer of the Globe Theatre, Shaftesbury Avenue, where a play of his was being rehearsed. When they broke for lunch he appeared with Ronnie Squire. They both looked at me with detached, quizzical amusement. I know now they felt rather put out: I was real; Freddy had got to do something about me.

It was not in any way a close, emotional, father-and-daughter scene. At the most this longed-for meeting took five minutes. He did not ask me for lunch; I cannot have been very attractive. I went away feeling dreadfully alone, but with Freddy's promise that he would speak to a Mr Barry O'Brien, and an instruction to write to the power behind that scene, Miss Ena Lovell, for an appointment.

The successful plays of an American writing for the London stage, Walter Hackett, went on tour with rather good companies and were presented by Barry O'Brien. They were whodunnit comedies written for Hackett's wife, Marian Lorne, but there was, of course, in each play an ingénue. I did as I was told. It worked. I was seen. Ena Lovell was a small, dark, pretty, rather bossy woman. She appeared to do all the work, certainly all the casting. In London the ingénue was played by a beautiful, new young actress called Diana Wynyard, and on tour by Angela Worthington. The Marian Lorne parts in the touring company were in the hands of Doris Rogers.

All over the provinces I played the same girl, in plays with different names but demanding very similar performances. The one I remember most was *The First Mrs Fraser* by St John Ervine, which we rehearsed at the Haymarket Theatre where the great Marie Tempest was the leading lady. This time I was playing the part taken in London by Ursula Jeans. I was amused when

I had to sit on a chair down-stage and found the chair was nailed to the floor. When we finished rehearsing I ran into the stage manager of the company. 'Why is that chair nailed to the floor?' He laughed. 'Miss Tempest would never risk a young actress moving one inch up-stage.'

The leading lady on tour in *The First Mrs Fraser* was Iris Hoey. I rather admired her but she could not stand me. I was getting prettier and better at the job, but I was having too good a time. I began to have admirers. They left flowers and messages at the stage door – 'Would I take supper?' All that seems a bit dated now but it went straight to my head and I was in pretty high spirits. This turn of events enraged Iris, who all her life had worked hard and was now coming to the end of the road. So she made life very difficult for me and I got the sack. Indiscipline was the charge and no doubt there was an element of truth in it. I went back to my 'good address' to lick my wounds and tidy my rather sparse wardrobe while sorting out what to do next.

I started to have a busy social life in London, far better than girls officially brought out and presented at Court, as was the custom. Glitters took an approving line because she rather cynically thought marriage essential, for a 'start in life' at least. She knew that the first step might not be the last and she referred to it as 'a good jumping off point'. Thus suitable young men must be entertained at the home of her admired daughters – 'so important they see a good background'.

This presented several hurdles. The good address was quite well equipped: she had salvaged from Birchington bits of her best furniture and her good taste had, of course, not deserted her. But while the household was tidy, it was shabby and, worst of all, we were nearly always broke. Often she pawned the silver, with the help of a 'gentleman near Victoria Station', to provide the necessities of life and so when possible marriage partners accepted the invitation to dine there would be, amid much laughter, a whip-round to raise enough to get the silver back. It was called 'Keeping our end up – it's Georgian, you know' and we made no secret of it, indeed I 'dined out' on that sort of story. We thought Glitters most courageous and funny at those moments.

Another quirk of hers was the manner in which she would judge these young men. Of course, they must have good manners and breeding, must be courteous, preferably amusing too, or they would be referred to as 'oafs' or, worse still, 'go-bos'. But above all they must, absolutely must, wear hand-made shoes, the name Lobb really being the name to set the only standard she required. No matter how eligible a beau might be, if the shoes were not right for her, she would dismiss him as unsuitable. She would forget his name and in a scornful voice refer to him as 'Lotus and Delta'.

None of this was resented by us, I presume because although we quite liked a number of these young men I do not remember any of us thinking we were in love.

*

During my time in Primrose Hill, I discovered how much I liked being alone. My room was clean and bright, with small windows looking out over Primrose Hill; it was heated by a gas fire, and I could very nearly always find a shilling for that. The bed was comfortable. The only meal I took was a cooked breakfast, served in the dining room where I would observe my fellow guests. I can only remember two of them and I cannot imagine what they were doing in this boarding house. One was Ernest Milton, a good actor who never really became the star he should have been, and the other was a lady I understood was his wife; since she was immensely respectable-looking, this was probably so.

I never made friends, however, because immediately after breakfast I set out on foot to the nearest underground station where I boarded the train for Gower Street and RADA. I would have preferred to stay in Primrose Hill rather than rejoin my family, but cheap as it was, it was more than Glitters could afford.

However, my evening occupation was far from solitary, and

had I been a boy and not a seventeen-year-old girl, would have been called sowing wild oats. I was not exactly promiscuous – flattery not sex was my main interest – but I was lazy, and it was often easier to say yes than to say no. There were few troubles that I avoided from being so vain, silly and slip-shod. The real reason I found myself in such plights was my innocence, and yet that was the last word ever applied to me.

A particular friend of mine was Sylvia Coke, a pretty, plump girl, the first of my friends Glitters referred to as 'fast'. Even later, when my steady boyfriend was Hugo Rignold, I enjoyed going out at night with quite a lot of young men, because my boyfriend's working hours were from 9 p.m. to 2 a.m. I never told him and many of these friendships remained, for the most part, quite platonic; they were very enjoyable and we would dance all night. A theory of mine then, and now, is that sometimes men are rather grateful if they do not feel they have to make a pass.

I do not find the London scene today very different from the one which, due to Sylvia's introductions, I was leading then. In those days, however, either my escorts were very rich or the only big change that has come about is in the economics of London night life. We roamed from the Florida, in a mews off Berkeley Square – the chief attraction there was the telephones linking every table, so that tremendous romances would start with the stranger 'across a crowded room' – to the Café Anglais in Leicester Square, and then wander arm-in-arm not far to Chez Henri in Long Acre, to hear the matchless black singer, Hutch, sing love songs to us, accompanying himself on the piano. When he sang, no one wanted to go home.

Two men I remember, John Heygate and Ewart Garland, were a good deal older than me and took me to parties in Chelsea where drugs were openly handed round. Cocaine was the one most referred to. For the most part I was inclined to sit on the fence, in the role of observer. I was certainly offered drugs but never accepted even a sniff of anything. This was not because I was a good or disciplined girl. I had not the faintest need of any stimulant and therefore no understanding of those who did. I saw what happened to people whose temperaments were the opposite to my own: most of them have not survived to reminisce with me. My later intolerance and lack of understanding when my son, James, got caught up in the drug scene stemmed, I'm sure, from those days.

My first really queer friend was a fat boy, very rich and very generous, called Gussie Schweder; he had a flat in Curzon Street where he entertained continually the young jetset of our day. He was an outrageous, decadent boy but with a good heart. Like many others I accepted his hospitality and, as far as I can remember, gave nothing in return except to enjoy myself at his expense, so I felt a real blow to the heart when, not so very long ago, I was about to brush aside the efforts of a tramp in Knightsbridge who tried to sell me flowers. I did stop to buy a bunch, and the eyes that looked at me from a ravaged face were Gussie Schweder's. Spontaneously I said, 'Gussie!' and in my embarrassment started to walk away. Then I turned back. He must have been used to encountering old acquaintances, because he said at once, 'Be off with you!'

When I was eighteen I fixed up to go to Southend Repertory Theatre for a season. This was great fun. I shared digs with some Wall of Death riders who were doing a season at the Kursaal. They were a team of rough, working-class boys and girls. I thought them extremely brave and whenever I could I watched their act and their rehearsals. When I expressed wonder at their skill they laughed and explained that all you needed to be was a good mechanic and have a good machine. Provided the engine did not fail, no problem. If it did they knew they faced dreadful injury, probably death.

Then a better offer came from the Bristol Little Theatre to do a whole repertory season, opening with a new play by Eden Phillpotts, who had written the great success called *Yellow Sands*. The new play was entitled *Buy a Broom*. It was awful, so was I, but a busy, rather successful time followed, with me playing the leading young girl parts. Growing somewhat less dedicated and a bit bored at weekends, I lived alone in digs with a Bristol family: the husband worked in the Will's tobacco factory. I had a very simple bedroom and the use of the front parlour, complete with aspidistra, all for a pittance, but I much preferred eating with the family in the kitchen. I learned a great deal about what it meant to work in a tobacco factory; 'Dad' was often too tired to eat after his awful day working for little money.

When, at weekends, a tempting invitation in London turned up, I would rush from the theatre to the station to catch the last train. This was not too popular with the director of the theatre, but I was undeterred. By the skin of my teeth I would make it, usually leaping on to the train as it was moving. I would find that everything was ready at the good address just for me to sneak in and go to bed.

The object of my first great affection was a musician named Hugo Rignold. When I was about thirteen I had first seen him playing first violin in Hylton's Band: in those days big bands were the rage and Jack Hylton's was a household name. I had worshipped steadfastly from a distance.

One Saturday night after my dash from the theatre I found a first-class carriage – the London train was packed – knowing and not caring for once that I must pay the difference. I was making an effort to heave my suitcase on to the luggage rack, when a man sitting opposite offered to help. It was Hugo Rignold.

From that moment on my life changed. I loved him in reality as much as I had in my imagination, and to my amazement he was ready to assure me that he loved me too. He was the most attractive man I have ever known. He was amusing, and had a great sense of comedy on the stage. He really understood jazz, of which I had very little knowledge or appreciation, although it was the music I enjoyed most.

Hugo had come from Winnipeg in Canada because he had won a scholarship at the Royal College of Music. He was a very good violinist and musically a very talented young man, but I do not know whether he could ever have been in the first flight of concert performers. I do know that he was hard up, which is why he took the job with Hylton's band.

A fellow student of his at the RCM had been a girl called Maxine Hyman, and she had taken Hugo home to her family sometimes for weekends. Walter Hyman, whom Hugo referred to with much affection as a rag-and-bone-man, was very kind and like a father took him under his wing. Walter realized that, even with Jack Hylton, Hugo was going to earn, with concerts, plus recordings, quite a lot of money, so he became responsible for his finances, allowed him twenty pounds a week and invested the rest. The Hymans were a happy, prosperous family with a home at Rickmansworth, and until he met us I think they were the only personal friends Hugo had made in England. He brought me to see them soon after we met. Maxine and her sister were friendly girls, and Sundays there were great fun.

Hugo was a hard worker who enjoyed life. My family were fond of him. It was quite impossible not to like or love him but even so there was never one moment when I had the faintest intention of marrying him, nor do I think he wanted to marry me, although he was a decent man and sometimes felt he ought to.

Apart from his finely shaped, blue eyes, Hugo's features were, I often thought, negroid and so, when he had finally saved enough money to bring his sister, Bubbles, to England, and a rather plain, undeniably black, girl got off the train, I was not a bit surprised; nor did it worry me in any way. I have always found black people attractive and I love the music they make. I took Bubbles to meet my mother, who used that awful expression 'A touch of the tarbrush, dear.'

'Touch, Mummy, is the understatement of the year.'

This was the sort of joke Hugo liked and I remember him giggling. Of course he was not a saint and had the usual areas of selfishness: he was devoted to his Bugatti. He would spend hours in garages discussing or fiddling about with the engine, and every free moment we had was spent watching the racing at Brooklands. That was my idea of Hell but Hugo never noticed and would have paid no attention anyway. Despite the Bugatti obsession, no girl has ever been happier than I was with Hugo while our affair lasted. Because of him, I formed a very good view of men in general. He introduced me to romance, to fun, and affection. Shortly before he died we met again, and I told him, gratefully, of this good deed. He had returned successfully to the world of classical music, becoming the conductor of the Liverpool Philharmonic; when my son James was, as a child actor, making the film of *The Magnet* in Liverpool, I took him to see Hugo conduct.

But Hugo was in no way suitable; his shoes were quite, quite wrong. When I moved into his London flat, Glitters always kidded herself that I was not living with him. 'Not really,' she would say, 'she doesn't care for that sort of thing.' Glitters had a habit that I found very tiresome, of discussing her daughters in front of people, sometimes even when the daughter in question was present. But I used to smile when she would regale her friends with stories about my relationships, sometimes even my success, with men, happy in the knowledge that she was pretty well one hundred per cent wrong when she would lay down dogmatic facts. 'Angela is very attractive to men, but she is not faintly interested in going to bed with any of them.' This was when I was living with Hugo. Later on, I heard her say that I had an enormous success with the opposite sex and that men were always travelling across the world to see me. More often than not they were just good friends who needed somewhere to stay.

Yet, to be fair to her, when Hugo and I were drifting apart she did very firmly find a way of getting me invited to Switzerland to spare me the pain of parting from him. She saw him as soon as I had gone, and somehow persuaded him to have the courage to write and tell me he wanted to marry a friend of mine, about whom I had been shedding jealous tears for some time. I received this letter at the beautiful house at Territet where I was staying with some friends called Feraldo. Alone in my bedroom I did a lot of crying, railed against my mother's 'bloody interference', then dried my eyes and admitted to myself that she was absolutely right – I never wanted to marry him and had always refused to do so. In fact Hugo was the marrying kind: he did it three or four times after we parted.

*

Before our parting Hugo and I had been inseparable. He liked to be the one to earn the money. He worked very hard recording as well as playing in the band, and I used to hang around and be ready to do whatever interested him or amused him in his free time. I had fulfilled, but half-heartedly, my contract at Bristol: acting had become neglected while the sun rose and set on my obsession for Hugo. For a while he had accepted my being at Bristol, and would even drive me back there sometimes on Monday in his terrifying Bugatti. Sometimes he would tell me that he would be broadcasting, and that he would be playing certain things especially for me. This would be the high-spot of our evening in the Bristol kitchen. There was one tune in particular that he played, I don't know its name, but I hum it very often and know just a few of the words: 'At the sound of your voice heaven opened its portals to me'. This was considered very romantic and we would all swing and sway together in the kitchen. It *was* romantic, though 'portals' seemed overdone, even then.

One day before my contract had come to an end, between a matinée and evening performance, the girls who shared my dressing-room and I tossed a coin to decide who would go out and buy the buns we stuffed ourselves with between performances. It was my turn and in haste, not attending to what I was doing, I was nearly run over. There was the usual screeching of brakes and hooting. I was starting to apologize when my 'Sorry, I'm so sorry, all my fault' turned to screams of delight because two girl-friends from RADA were in the back. Traffic was held up quite a bit while introductions were made.

The girls were Sylvia Coke and Barbara Waring. The man

passenger in front was John Emery-Jones, editor of the *Bristol Evening World*. The driver, a small, tubby Jewish boy in glasses, said his name was Michael Sieff.

They came to the play that night, and I knew at once that John Emery-Jones was ready at least to enjoy a flirtation with me, to sound out his chances; but it was Michael Sieff who subsequently came again and who spent a fortune on flowers for me, playing to perfection the 'stage-door Johnny'. I did not understand why this should be so, but I was amused and we made friends. Michael told me he had a very humble job learning the business in a local branch of some store called Marks & Spencer: his father, Israel Sieff, had married Rebecca, daughter of Michael Marks, the founder of the chain. He also told me he was engaged to a girl called Daphne Michael, but this never stopped the flow of flowers and flattery he bestowed on me. I had never heard of the Sieffs and imagined Michael as a hardworking boy in some small family concern.

When I returned to London, this attention continued. Hugo did not mind at all – with good reason: he was very sure of me and Michael was not attractive-looking. He was the eldest of Rebecca and Israel Sieff's children, but I think he really always lived in the shadow of his brother, Marcus, their second son. Marcus was handsome, dynamic, ambitious, a born tycoon. Michael was short, squat and balding very early on, with thick glasses which he always referred to as his 'brillies', but he was sweet and companionable. Of all the family Michael was the only one with a really irresistible charm, linked to a huge enjoyment of the good things of life. There was something of the naughty boy in his personality. His passion was pretty women. But he was lovable and whatever tricks he got up to, he was always forgiven.

Michael was forever asking me out and wanted me to meet his mother and father. I always refused, thinking he was being ridiculous and that he really should stop spending money on me that I was sure he couldn't afford. Finally, encouraged by Hugo, who was working then until 2 a.m. at the Savoy, in Carroll Gibbons' Savoy Orpheans, I accepted Michael's invitation.

Hugo had told me I was being mean to the little man, and snobbish, and that I didn't think he was good enough. On the night I did consent to go out with Michael, a magnificent car drew up at our lodgings in Old Quebec Street – Michael knew I was living with Hugo. Hugo saw the car. 'There,' he said, 'I knew you should go, the poor fellow has even hired a huge car to impress you.'

The car, of course, belonged to Michael's father and we drove to the fabulous family home in Sussex Square, Regent's Park. His father was, in fact, joint head with Simon Marks of Marks & Spencer. Michael had never told me this; he was modest but also, I suspect, he just took the family for granted. I was greeted by my hostess for the evening, his mother, Rebecca, the most beautiful Jewish woman I have ever seen. 'Very Old Testament' was how I described her to Glitters.

Rebecca held herself with dignity. She had dark hair parted in the middle. It was long and was caught in a chignon on the nape of her neck. She had wonderful, heavy-lidded blue eyes, and wore very fine jewellery, the like of which I had never seen. She and Israel greeted me warmly. The dinner party was huge and the guests included distinguished people from all walks of life.

The young members of the family and their friends had a table to themselves, at which I sat. I remember Marcus Sieff, and Daphne, Michael's fiancée, very clearly. And sitting next to me was a good-looking young man. 'Why are you here?' he asked. 'You look as if you didn't belong.'

'I don't, but Michael has been kind to me, and my mother was strict and said that if I accepted invitations I must never back out. Why are you here?'

'I didn't want to come either. I wanted to go on a bender with my brother. But I'm Daphne's cousin. My mother is strict, too. She said I had accepted, so I must come.'

His name was Robin Fox.

3

The Foxes of Finchley Road

In the 1930s north of the Park and south of the Park were two different worlds and Robin's mother, Hilda Fox, and Glitters were prime examples of this difference. Nevertheless they had one thing in common: a firm belief that if all else failed, their children would get by on good manners. Had Robin and I not been dragooned by these strong ladies into what was termed by both as 'pulling your weight' we might not have met, and our sons, Edward, James and Robert, might never have been born. My mother constantly referred to 'Casting your bread upon the waters' but Hilda was half Jewish and had not got round to reading the New Testament, so her instructions to her children read: 'You will do as I say' – and they did. Soon after we met, Robin invited me home to 79 Finchley Road where his mother, now divorced, lived with four children ranging from their early twenties to fourteen – Mary, Kenneth, Robin and Pamela.

Hilda's husband's full name was Arthur William Fox, and he was the surviving son – his elder brother had been killed steeplechasing – of a self-made millionaire and three times Mayor of Harrogate called Samson Fox, a man born in conditions of the utmost poverty who went on to found Leeds Forged Steel. Among other enterprises, Samson had invented the corrugation of iron, and the bogey wheel which made the great American railways a reality. He had also found time for many hobbies: he was a master at driving a four-in-hand, he carved delicately in ivory, and he developed a knowledge and love of music, becoming a good amateur violinist. He built the Royal College of Music in Kensington. In appearance Samson had been a short, stocky man, a tough, bearded red-head with a strong Yorkshire accent. He invited his friends to a huge party to meet his bride-to-be – no ladies were allowed to be present – and when the parlour-maid came into the dining-room to serve them he rose to his feet, interrupted the proceedings, and announced that she was the lady he was going to marry. What this entirely self-educated and strong individual wanted most for his remaining son and heir was that he should become a real English gentleman. The family crest is a fox going like hell over a piece of corrugated iron.

When I arrived at Finchley Road, Hilda and Willie had been divorced for seven years. During their marriage Willie had conducted flirtations in front of Hilda with her friends and after a good many scenes she had come to terms with this; after all, they had a fine house in London, in Stratton Street, a house on the river at Sonning, while for the shooting Bolton Abbey was rented from the Duke of Devonshire and Blair Atholl from the Duke of Atholl. There was ample provision of good servants – both for indoors and outdoors – and trips abroad whenever the mood took them. Willie had never done a stroke of work in his life but he was a born organizer, and even this life lived entirely for pleasure would not have run smoothly without an efficient man at the helm. Hilda, quite naturally, basked happily, even complacently, in all that luxury and had decided that she must put up with his philanderings. She could be reasonably secure in the knowledge that they were not serious, and that he would not leave her.

But she was proved wrong on this last point, for suddenly, with no warning signs, her life and her children's happiness, she believed, had been shattered. Willie met again someone to whom he had been attracted many years earlier, the American-born Edna Lewishon, who had once been Diamond Jim Brady's mistress. The temptation was too great, her beauty and huge fortune proved irresistible. He became so besotted with her that even his children were forgotten. Soon after they were married, however, she died of appendicitis.

Altogether Hilda had borne Willie five children, the first of which had been stillborn. By the time I met her, she had taken on a role that she played to perfection, that of the cruelly treated, faithful wife, deserted and left entirely alone by a wastrel and a philanderer to bring up four beloved children in dire straits. She referred to her very generous allowance as 'a pittance'. Having got used to the former life, she did feel very insecure, and much of her considerable energy was now spent scheming and planning to make sure that her children would never, never leave her. She also spent much time telling and retelling stories of the fantastic luxury she had shared with their father and how good she had been to him – and how she had been rewarded – constantly reviling their father to her impressionable and quite kind-hearted children.

As an outsider, I was fascinated by her, and never grew tired of listening: I was particularly amused because she had a passion and violence I had not encountered before. The impression I gained of Willie Fox – probably because I had not been involved – had other aspects to it, and I rather looked forward to meeting the wicked fellow.

I was at Finchley Road a lot because it was at this time that my affair with Hugo Rignold was drawing to a close. Robin and his brother, Ken, knew that Hugo and I were getting on badly, and would discuss my problem and slight sadness by the hour, teasing me, and giving me their advice. Some of it was sound, even though they were young.

Robin was training to become a solicitor, and was articled to Simmonds and Simmonds, a big firm in the City. Getting a start there had been manoeuvred by Hilda, a life-long friend of the twins who were the senior partners. One of the first things Robin told me about his job linked with a conversation I had had with Glitters when we walked back from the theatre and she had told me about Clarence Hatry. Robin had to take papers to Maidstone

Jail for Hatry to sign. This man impressed him as he did everybody, and Robin had been fascinated to see the library he had created to be enjoyed by the prisoners and the garden he had just begun making around the prison.

Robin's first love was the theatre. Since childhood he had wanted to be an actor but Hilda had been adamant that he must have a profession, and as by then she held the purse strings and only parted with a penny if things were going her way, he was caught in a maternal trap. To be fair, Hilda knew a great deal about the theatre, having been an actress herself and having started work at fourteen for a few shillings a week: this was all she had had by way of education. She and her sister, Lily, had achieved fame as the Hanbury sisters; both had been Beerbohm Tree's leading ladies; Lily had been a great beauty but although Hilda had good looks, she did not match Lily. By the time I began my friendship with Robin, Hilda was a handsome, rather overweight woman, aquiline in features, with brown eyes – sharp at seeing what she wished to see – and magnificent, snow-white hair.

I don't know if Glitters had seen that Robin might possibly make a good husband for me: she may well have been more aware of his real feelings towards me than I was. Certainly she never complained about my being with the Foxes a great deal, although from the moment they met our two mothers fell prey to mutual dislike. Hilda had embraced social convention – it was her armour – while Glitters had remained outside it, only using it when it could be of advantage. Glitters admitted that Hilda 'made a very good home' for her children but before long it became known that Hilda referred to my mother as 'That Woman'. I think the thing she feared and suspected most was our lack of money.

Hilda had always had good servants, priding herself on the fact that she could not boil an egg and had no intention of learning how to. Of course she could take credit for the fact that the house was well-run, but her real cleverness lay in choosing the right servants: no matter what the political climate of the day they stayed with her and were devoted and loyal. One of her hobbies was shopping, which she did at Selfridges because she found the food department easily the best in London. Every morning she could be seen there walking round as if she owned the store, and she was always whistling. Selfridges never had a better customer, so she was entitled to this small eccentricity. Another hobby was bridge, and she gave at least one dinner party a week, followed by a game at one or two tables. The standard of play, though not the stakes, was high and Robin was encouraged to play quite often – he became very good and enjoyed the game all his life.

Willie had been a good father, unusual for a man in that position. His children had been taught everything by experts who had, in turn, been supervised by him: the second-rate was not tolerated. When I first met Robin, I used to enjoy trying to find out what he could not do. He was outstanding at tennis, golf and cricket – he and his brother had been put down for the MCC at birth (a custom Robin followed with his own three sons). He had swum for Harrow; I have never seen a man dive better, or from greater heights. He was an excellent shot – Willie was known to be as good as King George V, one of the best shots in the kingdom – and a skilful fisherman. He loved to take out a punt on the river – even I could enjoy that, listening to 'If You Knew Suzie' or 'All Alone on the Telephone' played on the wind-up gramophone. Willie it was who taught his children to play bridge and poker – 'teach them to judge character' was his attitude to this. He taught them backgammon too.

The Fox children of Robin's generation had nannies and governesses but they were with their parents a great deal, so as a result they were never awkward with grown-ups. Robin when I met him was like me only eighteen; but, though not precocious, he was a young man of the world, at least with women, who danced gracefully and spoke French so well it was difficult to believe that he was English. Perhaps the only lack was that Willie and Hilda had brought nothing intellectual to his background, although they did have a good ear for, and appreciation of, music.

When I first arrived at Finchley Road, Hilda was on the point of losing her elder son, Ken, who loved and wanted to marry Lord Decie's daughter, Eileen. By devious and cruel means, including the interception of vital love letters, she succeeded in preventing this, and so spoiled both their lives. She reaped a just reward, however. On the rebound Ken married a girl from his office, with whom neither Hilda nor her family ever shared a thought or word in common. His family found it hard to come to terms with the fact that these two stayed together for many years, in fact until she died, and clearly he needed her, even loved her, and of course their children.

If Hilda had her own way, the family often dined at home, inviting their friends if they must. At 10 p.m. the parlour-maid brought in a heavy silver tray: china tea and rich fruit cake were served before 'Goodnight, Madam' – Hilda thought she was very democratic, allowing the servants to go to bed then. In fact she curtailed the evenings by insisting that her family pour the last whiskies and help her guests on with their coats, and see them to their chauffeur-driven cars. All this was quite fun, partly at least because she did have a Jewish turn of humour which I came to love. My own great-grandmother on Glitters' side was Portuguese Jewish, and somehow to me this link between my family and Robin's became important. Jewish people were the only people Hilda loved and she always referred to them as KGs, Common Jews: 'Tell me about him, Hilda.' 'Ah, my dear, a good kind man if ever there was one, and one of the finest KGs who ever lived.'

She had known Marie Tempest well: they had a strong mutual dislike of each other. I once said to Hilda, 'She's not as black as you paint her. She took the trouble to teach Ursula Jeans six-pack bezique; they were often up all night.'

'Naturally,' she snapped, 'having already lost her own looks she's going to do her best to ruin those of a younger woman.' Hilda was always well groomed and wore fine furs and jewels – diamonds and pearls were her line – and her knowledge of these luxuries, which she passed on to Robin, was expert. She told me that from the time Robin was very small her clothes had been made by Reville, and he loved to go with her to all the fittings.

*

Robin's and my greatest friend was still Michael Sieff, and this had Hilda's blessing. For one thing 'His family are all good KGs, you know . . . and not too orthodox.' This last thought put Hilda at ease because, although her sympathies were Jewish, she never, as far as I can remember, went near a synagogue. Although Willie was not Jewish, he and Hilda must have decided not to argue about religion – I never heard of Willie entering a church, except for his own funeral.

Michael's fiancée, Daphne Michael, was a second cousin of Hilda's, a further reason for pleased smiles in the family circle. Daphne's mother, Nora Kerin, like the Hanbury sisters in Beerbohm Tree's Company, had been a household name and picture-postcard beauty. Reigning queen of the theatrical side of the whole family, however, was another cousin, Julia Nielson-Terry, a blazing personality with fabulous looks. She was a superb hostess to us all.

Julia's husband was Fred Terry, whom I remember as one of the most accomplished and charming actors I shall ever see. The great-uncle of John Gielgud, he deserves to be remembered as one of the great actors like Kean, Garrick, and Irving; but he is not talked about much today, perhaps because his great talent was curbed by the fact that glorious Julia never let him out of her sight if she could help it which, from her point of view, was possibly wise. She also insisted that she should always be his leading lady – and she was simply terrible. They toured the big provincial theatres for many years, mostly in *The Scarlet Pimpernel.* His immaculate performances had charm, style, and an authority which for me has seldom, if ever, been matched, his interpretation being the exact opposite of what is succeeding today. On their travels they indulged their hobby of collecting antique furniture, which in those days they could buy for little money. As a result their home near Regent's Park had become a warm and over-crowded museum. Julia was generous and gave me some lovely things. It seemed to me that everything, even the lobsters they served, were larger than life. They had a huge, blonde daughter, also an actress, called Phyllis. The talk and laughter at dinner was noisy and amusing, and entirely about the theatre – nothing else was worth mentioning. This was life.

Another theatrical family close to the Foxes were the du Mauriers, Gerald and Muriel, Angela, Daphne and Jeanne. I was taken to play tennis at Cannon Hall in Hampstead where they lived, and thus met up again with the friends I had made at Birchington when Harry was their doctor. Gerald was the conventional father on these occasions; for him and Muriel, the great event was tea after tennis on Sunday. Their home was like a stage set for the latest Lonsdale comedy: the scones, cakes, jam, honey, were all home-made and we would come in from tennis and clear the table like locusts, which pleased Muriel very much. She was a sweet and pretty woman, and Gerald treated her as if he had just that moment for the first time set eyes on her and fallen deeply in love. He used to tell us often – and seriously – that this was *the* way to treat your marriage partner.

Sometimes I was invited by the Foxes to stay with the American millionaire, Howard Jay Gould; his English house was Mongewell Park, near Wallingford, and during summer weekends he lived here, entertaining his own generation and his and their children's friends. During the week he lived in London at the Ritz. The luxury bestowed on us at Mongewell was of such a high order that looking back I am ashamed to think how we all took it for granted.

Howard had been born a millionaire but he often told me that this gave him no satisfaction: he actually envied people who had to work for their living, he said. There is little doubt that had he put envy to the test and pursued a career, he would have been successful: his estate was run so efficiently I cannot think of one detail of care or comfort that was missing. There was something to amuse all ages, all tastes: tennis, with a professional always in attendance; swimming, in a magnificent indoor pool; a nine-hole golf course; croquet. Around 6 p.m., when the first cocktails were served, we would all go to the bowling alley where we would play until it was time to dress for dinner. For those who liked violent exercise – like Robin and his brother – there was a squash court; and there was stické – a fast and exciting game which had originated in India, a cross between squash and real tennis.

Howard had a wonderful chef, too, and each day during the summer months the head gardener brought in the best English vegetables and soft fruits – raspberries, strawberries, melons, peaches. I was never as keen on bowls as at looking at the gardens, so in the evenings, with Howard's daughter, Ronda, I would wander through the kitchen garden, and the peach and grape houses. We spoilt girls would then go to our rooms to find our hot baths had already been drawn for us, our evening dresses laid out; wirelesses played in the bedrooms and bathrooms, in case we should suffer one second's boredom. All we were asked to contribute to those extraordinary weekends was to 'pull our weight', in other words to join in activities from breakfast to bedtime – and write 'Thank You' letters the moment we left.

I was particularly close to Ronda. Her mother was a well known American actress called Doris Keane, famous in London for her role in *Romance*. When I first knew Howard his beautiful lady love was the fabulous Edna May – the 'Belle of New York' – but Doris Keane was often at Mongewell at the same time; it was all very friendly. These wonderful ladies would slowly descend the staircase at dinner time, dressed by, perhaps, Molyneux, Balmain, or Mainbocher, according to their mood, and wearing jewellery such as we never see today – appearing in no way overdressed, just perfect of their type, and hell-bent on outshining each other. To be beautiful in itself requires great discipline; Howard loved the show – and of course he paid the bills. It made him chuckle. Howard had no looks at all. He was a small, fat fellow.

One night Howard told me that since he first came to England he had been friends with Hilda and Willie Fox, and felt it was high time they stopped being so childish towards each other. Willie was alone in Paris: now it seemed to Howard that Willie and Hilda should meet. When we discussed what I had been told of Willie's reprehensible behaviour, Howard smiled and shrugged his shoulders: 'Ladies are inclined to exaggerate, my dear.' Howard also thought that I should meet Willie: if the rest of the family was so prejudiced against him, he suggested, then I could make it possible for Robin to know his father again. He was sure I would get on with Willie. All this made very good sense and I asked Howard to invite Robin and me for dinner at the Ritz next time Willie was in London.

On receiving this invitation, Willie immediately reversed it, asking us to dine with him at Quaglino's in Bury Street, a hotel he had decided to patronize in order to judge if it came up to his standards.

So I went amiably and light-heartedly out to meet this old rascal I had heard so much about. I had nothing much else to do, being, in fact, at a rather loose end, although I did not realize it. Willie did realize it, and while he rather liked me – I think I amused him – he also saw at a glance that if Robin married me it would infuriate Hilda. When I think of the venom they poured out on one another, I cannot but believe that something equally strong – great passion and mutual need – must have existed between them in their early years together. But now Willie was bored, a shrewd man capable of using strength and his legendary charm to manipulate people, to get his own way – but for what? Just to sit back and enjoy the effect.

At Quaglino's he greeted us both with warmth and affection as if he had always known us, as if he and Robin had been together just yesterday. He dressed most elegantly but in an understated way; he was often named in magazines as the best-dressed man in the world. This didn't affect him much, though he knew perfectly well that it was true. In those first moments, casually and with ease, he established a relationship with Robin and myself that lasted till his death. It wasn't difficult to gauge Robin's thoughts. He wanted me to go down well with 'Dad' – he came at once to address his father thus – after all, in his inner self he had always loved him deeply. From then on 'Dad' could do no wrong, while the umbilical cord with his mother began to be severed. The Foxes were really men's men; women were vitally necessary but as ornaments chiefly – to be turned to when the day's business and fun were over. Women were considered to exist to please, to comfort and amuse their men – and if they failed, the men left them. It was up to the women to see that the financial settlements were to their liking – a hard code, perhaps, but that's how they were.

*

From the moment we met Willie at Quaglino's, until the outbreak of war, when he disappeared first to Lisbon and then to New York, Willie dominated our lives. Of course he wanted his good-looking, companionable son with him as much as was possible, and perhaps he felt this could only happen provided Angela came along too. At any rate, after that first dinner we were immediately invited to visit him in Paris, and I remember lying awake at night wondering how could I possibly manage: the thought of my inadequate wardrobe was the worst worry.

However, off we went to Paris, arriving at the lovely apartment in the Rue d'Artois off the Champs-Elysées where Willie's maid, Rose, unpacked my suitcase and with needle, cotton and an iron transformed my dresses from being 'good enough to get by in' into something quite out of the ordinary. Rose was the textbook Frenchwoman. I have seen real love on one or two occasions in my life, but the first time I was aware of this wonderful phenomenon was when I observed Rose's selfless devotion to her master, which came immediately to include Robin and myself.

I had never been to Paris before and it would be putting it mildly to say that I was thrown in at the deep end. Willie's evening haunts were exclusive and expensive restaurants where he was welcomed and adored by the great maîtres d'hôtels.

Before these, however, he and Robin would disappear to the Travellers' Club for some male gossip and high-powered games of backgammon and snooker, so I would at least have time to dress. After dinner my education began in earnest with, to break me in, visits to risqué night clubs, in particular to one called Le Monôcle, the lesbian hang-out. I began to learn, with some apprehension, of the decadent roué hidden behind Willie's famous charm. For his part, he perceived quite soon that much as I liked chatting to lesbians who were brought to the table, and thought them 'awfully nice', they were not my scene: in no way did I wish to leave the party to go and 'inspect the rooms upstairs'.

In no time at all brothels were on our visiting list: first, some cheap and jolly ones, patronized by the bourgeoisie, where dozens of stark naked girls would jog around dancing respectably to tinny music in front of ordinary French husbands and wives standing about drinking beer. When I asked Willie why they did this, he explained it was to excite the appetite of the customers. I expect he was right but I never noticed any glimmer of excitement in their eyes. Apart from the nakedness, it seemed rather a dull night out. But I giggled a lot, so I got promoted and was taken to the very exclusive brothels: the most famous of these was 13 Rue St Augustin. Here we were greeted by Madame herself, an elegant and sophisticated lady, who had champagne ready on ice. We were able to see, without being seen, a lot of seedy, silly old men choosing, from among a bonny-looking troupe circling in front of them, which girl was going to be responsible for their pleasure that evening. Willie used to know some of the men. It amused him hugely. Perhaps I was a prig but I was shocked. Still, that was nothing to the sense of shock I felt when later, in our friendly days, I told my mother-in-law of these evenings, saying, 'It's enough to put you off sex for life.'

'Oh,' said Hilda, 'I didn't feel that at all: I was rather ashamed because it always put me in the mood.'

Willie also had 'exhibitions' put on for Robin and me, always with two girls. I never graduated further than this. Apart from being deeply embarrassed – I thought what awfully bad luck on the girls – I grew bored, so when Willie wanted to stay talking with Madame, with whom he enjoyed conversation of an erotic nature, I persuaded the girls to show me over the building and explain what went on, enthusiastically asking questions in my appalling schoolgirl French. I found the girls delightful, most friendly towards me, and perfectly understanding towards my lack of desire to take part. I took the private address of one of them; we corresponded and later, when she married, I became godmother to her son. I once went to visit her in the 13th Arrondissement: I believe that not even the shrewdest of detectives would have seen a trace of the girl who was number one in popularity at 13 Rue St Augustin.

To this day I don't know whether Willie had marriage in mind for Robin and me, but he certainly did everything in his power to encourage us to live together, which we more or less drifted into. We were with him constantly in London and in Paris, or Biarritz or Le Touquet and, of course, for 'that precious week in Deauville' beloved by the very rich.

One of the results of our friendship was indeed that Hilda agreed to meet him again, though nothing further in the way of reconciliation took place subsequently. She even allowed the other children to be with him occasionally, and she unbent to the point of taking us to family evenings at the Savoy, too. I recall her, dressed in dark red velvet and diamonds, holding Robin's and Ken's hands, moving them up and down rhythmically to the strains of Carroll Gibbons' band, the Savoy Orpheans. I had to remain very straight-faced and not look at Carroll, whom I knew closely, for he had once been Hugo's best friend.

When we weren't at the 'chemmy' and baccarat tables with Willie, we were driving Hilda to weekends in Mongewell to see Howard Gould: as well as not being able to boil an egg, Hilda could not drive a car. She would even call us up to take her to see a friend she had a fancy to spend the day with in some other part of the country, with no regard for the fact that we might have plans of our own. Robin was her chauffeur and, like a chauffeur, he would wait all day until she was ready to be driven home, where there was always a good dinner waiting for us. Both she and Willie had, in their different ways, bought us.

Willie lavished hospitality on his family, even paying for Robin to have suits hand-made by his own tailor, Brinkman: the two of them would spend more hours than any woman choosing the correct materials. Their shirts were made in Paris by Lanvin: anything else would have been considered unwearable.

Thus Robin and I were caught in a pretty tight net. Even when we could escape from the family we were nearly always with the Sieffs. Michael's brother Marcus, now Lord Sieff, had become as close a friend as Michael. Israel and Rebecca had by this time set up residence at Sonning Park and took a lively interest in us. One always came away from their house stimulated and wanting to do better, not only for oneself but for other people too.

One particular problem featured largely in the conversation: the plight of the Jews in Germany. With the utmost discretion the Sieffs were using their power, influence and money to help people escape from the horrors of Nazism. Many people owed their lives to them: Judith Sieff married Konrad Steiner, one of the young German refugees helped by them to come to England. Others we met were Hans Schneider, a genius in the textile field who became responsible for Marks & Spencer's wonderful standards of design and colour; and a penniless world doubles tennis champion: Simon Marks helped him to a job by financing him in a factory which made sweets. He later became a millionaire industrialist, owning a string of race horses, and intensely generous to his country of adoption. Lilli Palmer, the actress, and her two sisters were brought out with Simon Marks's influence. The first time I ever met George Weidenfeld was in their house; his first marriage was to one of Edward Sieff's daughters.

It was because Michael and Daphne were going to get married that Robin and I decided that we would do the same: our joke was that Michael and Daphne could not possibly go on honeymoon without us. I cannot remember Robin being especially keen on the idea, so I always felt to some extent guilty; but I was suddenly determined that this was one hundred per cent what I wanted. I was determined to have children of my own and the only man I have ever set eyes on who I wished to be the father of my children was Robin Fox. That was so in 1934 and I would make exactly the same choice today. I never expected a man not to have faults but Robin's faults, even if some surprised me and often even pained me, were what I would rather live with than any other man's virtues. His qualities were what mattered, and I hoped my children would inherit a lot of them. I am lucky that they have: they are very, very like their father. He and I were entirely different in every way, starting in appearance. He was tall, dark, athletic and good-looking, with marvellous carriage and bearing. I was fair and funny – I don't know how else to see myself. We were always good companions, forever observing life together.

I used sometimes to think Robin was born mature, even sophisticated. That appealed to me, for he had a natural elegance and a fine appreciation of worldly things. But he was never a slave to possessions and therefore remained perfectly balanced when all luxury and beauty vanished. He found almost everything interesting but never wanted to do anything unless it could be done properly. His attitude to shooting demonstrated this exactly. He came quickly to accept that it was a sport he could not afford. 'We can't afford anything to do with it; neither can most of the men doing it today – they don't even know the rules of the game, the silly buggers have never been taught. They wouldn't know how to treat a loader if they had one, and they even clean their own boots!' In fact all his life he got great pleasure from simple country pursuits, rough shooting and fishing in particular, with his sister Mary and later with the boys. Another reason I liked him was because of his shrewdness about people, something I found then and find now very attractive. In all our years together, never once was he wrong.

Robin and I broke the news of our decision to marry, first to Willie, then to Hilda. Willie pretended to put up a few obstacles but Hilda literally shrieked and screamed and had hysterics – had she been a Victorian it would have been called The Vapours. Not only was I illegitimate, she pointed out, but I had no background, I was a whore and, moreover, extremely trivial; worse, I was the daughter of That Woman. 'All I've suffered! All I've sacrificed for my children!' I would make Robin's life miserable, she said – her beloved, adored son had fallen into the clutches of a feckless tramp. It was a very trying, frustrating, and exhausting time for everyone. Fortunately, however, impassioned though she was, Hilda was not very clever and my determination to marry Robin was greater than hers to stop me.

The night before the wedding my mother gave a big party at the Goring Hotel. Champagne was served and a string orchestra played: I cannot think how she got the money. All my friends, young and old, were invited and it was a lovely evening; we were still dancing at midnight.

The following morning, 31 October 1935, Robin and I were married at Caxton Hall. Willie had paid for the Hall to be very expensively decorated and I remember both families looking pretty good. Israel Sieff had given me a cheque for my wedding present and I had spent it on expensive clothes: a dress and coat of fine, smoke-blue wool. Robin looked his best in a new Brinkman brown suit. The best dressed woman there, as so often in those days, was Daphne Sieff. At the ceremony I remember, when we finally made our vows, looking at Hilda and thinking, 'Well, at least I'm stopping her doing to Robin what she did to Kenneth.' Of course, if you're young, lack of experience makes you rather hard: over the years I grew almost fond of my mother-in-law and learned to share a laugh with her.

As soon as we had signed the Register, we all set off for the bumper lunch that Willie was hosting in the Pinafore Room at the Savoy Hotel. I remember my mother, who detested him, sitting on his right, and Hilda, who hated him even more, sitting on his left. Willie was well aware of all this – it was the sort of situation that thoroughly amused him – and he played the great host with immense gusto and enjoyment.

Lunch over, we set out for Victoria Station where we caught the boat-train to Paris to begin our honeymoon, on which we were due to be looked after by Rose. Lord Ashfield, Chairman of the then Southern Railways, who was Robin's godfather, gave us as a wedding present a carriage to take us to Dover; here again we were spoilt with champagne, flowers and other presents. But my rake of a father-in-law, just before we set off, remarked, 'I don't think you've got any books.' He marched to the bookstall and returned with a novel, by Margaret Lane, entitled *Faith, Hope, and No Charity*.

4

Honeymoon and Battledress

The weather in Paris was beautiful. We stayed three days in a hotel near the Rue d'Artois, cossetted by Rosé. The following January we had Honeymoon Number Two at the Carlton in Cannes with Michael and Daphne Sieff. The Carlton was the favoured retreat of the Marks and Sieff family, and Robin and Michael's main desire on this second honeymoon was to play golf at Mougin every day; their evenings were given over to chemin de fer in the casino, while the brides had to amuse themselves as best they could.

To begin with at least, I savoured at the Carlton the height of its sophistication: I remember, for instance, meeting Michael Arlen, author of *The Green Hat*, the glamorous bestselling novel of the period; he joined us at the bar for a cocktail. For our generation he epitomized worldly success – an Armenian of small build, of sensitive manners and lonely disposition; he was married to a beautiful Greek called Atalanta but she never made an appearance.

Our first home was a small house in De Walden Street, off Marylebone High Street, a neat little nest for young socialites, where we had a live-in servant named Winnie. All seemed well, for the time being, at any rate, until the first balloon of our married life went up: the postman brought us news that Robin had failed his law finals. In fact, this was hardly surprising because he was only twenty-one and getting married young is

not exactly conducive to hard work; also, he spent a great deal
of time playing bridge and gambling for high stakes at the St
James's Club in Piccadilly, which then was exclusively a men's
club, but the blow pulled us up very sharp, and he mended his
ways, taking his finals again soon and passing.

When we had weathered this, it was my turn to become a
problem, to myself and to everyone else. I felt anonymous. Angela
Fox – who in God's name was she? I suffered again, as I had as
a child, bouts of really hysterical depression accompanied by a
strong desire to run away, made worse by the fact that I did not
know what I was running away from – or what I could run away
to. I was lost in the self-indulgent, worldly trappings of Hilda
and Willie, and the main trouble as I saw it was that although
there was a certain sort of fun to be had, provided one could
cope with the games people played, and although there was a
great deal of gossip, there was no communication. As a result
I felt enfolded, owned, by this group and out of touch with
my own family who had absolutely nothing in common with
them.

Yet it must have seemed to many people that I was leading an
enviable life: until 1939 we went with Willie on the rounds of
the smart resorts, visiting his rich old divorced friends, who were
much in need of company; in those days to be divorced meant
to be excommunicated. The divorced male had to take his
pleasures where he found them, as the price to be paid for
leaving and breaking up a home.

We would often run into the Duke of Windsor: this was the
beginning of his exile with Wallis Simpson, whom he had recently
married. Biarritz was their favoured resort. When we arrived
there, Willie immediately took Robin to play golf at Chiberta,
and I, the well-trained and ever-admiring walker of the course,
accompanied them. This golf club was the daily haunt of the
Duke. Willie thought the Royal clothes awful – and so they were:
very loudly checked tweed plus-fours, aggressively sporting black
and white shoes, the beret worn by French men in that part of
France. He looked like an Englishman who suddenly had enough

money to take an expensive holiday and was determined to play and dress the part, but despite all this effort he didn't appear quite at home.

When we arrived at the piscine cabin that Willie had hired through the hall porter at our hotel – in those days no one bathed in the sea at Biarritz – we found we were placed next door to the Windsors – so an amiable holiday friendship sprang up. Wallis was very much in command, clearly enjoying herself and providing rather good company – an intelligent American woman from Baltimore. Willie informed me, 'Quite good family as Americans go, better educated than most, but no money . . .' In America, that's not good news. My impression of the Duke was that he was caught between a desire to enjoy his new-found freedom and a regret that he did not receive the respect from courtiers that he and his family took for granted; as a result he was often caught on the wrong foot.

Wallis was not a great beauty, but she was attractive and vivacious, with great dress sense, as have so many American women living in Europe. I had known her slightly in London, as I had been taken several times to her flat of immaculate good taste in Bryanston Court when she was Mrs Simpson. An elegant, clever and tough woman of the world, she was neither clever enough nor tough enough to hold a candle to the ladies of the Duke's family left behind in England. When I met the Windsors in Biarritz my impression was not that she had fostered dreams of one day being Queen, but that she was quite certain they would be forgiven and that wounds would heal so that they would be able to make one of their homes in England. I was young and had never met a member of the Royal Family, but I was English and I knew for certain – by instinct, I suppose – that her wish would never come true.

In Biarritz she was popular with men, with whom she flirted and exchanged funny stories. We enjoyed a light-hearted holiday with them both. To women as well as to men she was easy on the eye, though she was a woman who reserved her energies for men far more than for other women. I can hear the laughter now, and the sound of the dice rattling on the backgammon board while she played.

Some years later my father-in-law took me to visit them in Paris. The house and garden were perfection. By this time it had been made all too clear to Wallis that she would not be accepted by the Royal Family. I found her a travesty of her former self: tremendously well-dressed and bejewelled still, but understandably embittered by her isolation. The Duke was washed out, snubbed and henpecked, a quarter of the man I had seen in Biarritz. And she was hell-bent on exercising her power. 'David, do this, David, do that.' He did as he was told. It may be difficult to imagine why but I felt more sorry for her than I did for him. She was so amazed, so disappointed by the hand that life had dealt her. After all, she went into the game high-spirited but unarmed, and he must have understood what the women he had known all his life would do to her: I saw her then as I see her now, a woman defeated by defeat.

*

Most summer holidays between 1935 and 1939 were spent with Hilda at Mawgan Porth, a bay in North Cornwall where every August she rented a seaside house. She used to go ahead with her maids Toddy and Laurie and her two daughters, Mary and Pamela. Then Ken and Eve, his wife, and Robin and Angela were summoned to Mawgan Porth: it was a command – I referred to it as 'Hilda's Balmoral'. Robin and I would arrive exhausted, having driven all night from London – he insisted this was more convenient – in Robin's Austin 7, always referred to as 'Austin'. On the narrow roads the journey seemed to take forever, but immediately we arrived our sophisticated, jet-set selves would melt or vanish, and almost before we greeted Hilda – and certainly before unpacking – on went our bathing dresses and we would dash down to the sea, shouting like children.

After this first swim Toddy would have ready for us porridge, bacon and eggs, sausages, coffee – so welcome after the 'petit

dejeuners' we had accepted from Willie. While we were eating
as fast as we could go, Robin and I would be telling Hilda what
we thought she should know about our time with her ex-husband.
Although I think I amused her, now she had come to accept
me a little more, I felt that all she really wanted was to be alone
with her family: for her Cornish visit, 'Mum', as Hilda was
called, wanted her children back – it recreated for her the only
feeling of safety that she had ever known. If they must bring
a wife or two with them, this was tiresome but just about tolerated.

On the Mawgan Porth beach she would sit under a parasol,
gazing at her young and their antics with an unchanging, seraphic
half-smile on her lips; yet her eyes were as watchful and as hard
as the diamond in the clasp of her pearls. She always wore the
same: well-cut beige linen skirt (wool in winter) and fine silk
blouse in soft colours. Diamonds enhanced the delicate and
pretty hand which held the parasol: no sun was allowed to touch
her complexion. Not a strand of her white hair seemed disturbed
by the breeze.

While the house Hilda rented was pleasant but quite ordinary,
the handsome younger Foxes, all four of them, had an air of
returning to ancestral lands. This attitude was not resented by
the locals; far from it, they seemed pleased to see them again
and had plans drawn up for deep sea fishing, bouts of local
wrestling (for Ken and Robin) and other 'sport', such as dynamit-
ing fish from under rocks.

The ancient art of Cornish wrestling was watched by Hilda.
The local men, reminding one of Spanish gypsies, were very
tough and their champion, Warne by name, had over the years
taught Hilda's boys to wrestle: I have no doubt he could have
broken all their bones whenever he chose, but his restraint was
admirable. I was a very nervous spectator. I would bite my fingers
until they bled, all laughter, even giggling, deserting me, knowing
for certain that Robin's back was about to be snapped. Hilda,
on the other hand, enjoyed every moment. Questioned afterwards
about her feelings she would answer, 'Do I feel nervous, is that

what you asked, dear? Nervous? What a funny word. My boys were wrestling, and of course they always win.'

For three weeks that first summer Robin played Happy Families to the hilt. He was the leader, the life and soul of the party, the most devoted son and brother in existence, and they adored him. He seemed to enjoy every moment, too, making his mother feel like a Cleopatra who had stayed young and not lost her Antony, clasping to her bosom not an asp but her youngest, beloved 'baby', Pamela. But as we drove away in Austin, even before the bay was out of sight, Robin's guise dropped away and I realized he did not really give a damn about any of them, particularly Hilda. He had tolerated the company of Mary and Ken, enjoyed stuffing Pamela with ice-cream and pocket-money, enjoyed all the sport and relaxation; but none of it remained with him.

For the first time I was made aware that he was capable of playing such a part; I remember my sense of shock. He drove for a long time without speaking, and I was given time to think about this strange man, and his family. Not only then, but at other times, I remained mystified about the nature of his real thoughts; he would never reveal them directly.

I speculated that inwardly he had remained deeply unhappy at his parents' breaking up, and had never really come to terms with it; that while his and his brother's and sisters' childhood had been as near idyllic as could be imagined, one day, during his early adolescent and most sensitive years, the happiness was quite suddenly over. I came to believe also that Robin never forgave his mother for, as he saw it, creating resentment towards his father, even driving him away, and that what heart Robin was left with belonged to his father. After the war Robin and I were unpacking his personal possessions and I found a huge pile of letters that bore his mother's handwriting: not one of them had been opened. By this time I knew him too well to comment, and I put the letters tidily away in a drawer, though I wondered why they had been kept at all. Somehow this treatment of his mother's letters summarized his attitude to women: although he needed them, he rejected their emotional behaviour. And his need for women and all they could give him was constant: he was attracted by them and amused by them, and he used, disliked and punished them.

*

When we had been married for about a year I became pregnant. We thought it normal and correct to tell Hilda first, and told her on holiday one brilliant summer's day. We had been swimming, sunbathing, laughing and talking with her on the golden beach of ribbed sands. The sea was far out, the tide playing no cruel and treacherous tricks when casually Robin said, 'Angela is going to have a baby.'

Hilda let out a scream, and screamed and screamed; amid this frantic hysteria we heard her call me a whore – and a syphilitic one at that – a wanton bitch who was destroying her son, a viper, and so on. It was shaming and disgusting. But somehow, because it had happened before, it was bearable, until she hit too low below my belt, and yelled at me that any child of mine would be born deformed and, 'Oh God, let it be born dead!'

It is quite possible that Hilda's violent outburst affected Robin more than I was capable of understanding. For this, if not some other reason, he shut himself off from me entirely. He still worked as a low form of life at Simmonds and Simmonds and in this capacity he obtained one day a licence to enable an American, Jules Stein, head of an entertainment agency called the Music Corporation of America, to open offices in London. For Robin to get this licence was just a routine job, but later his connection with MCA was to have a crucial effect on our lives.

Otherwise at this time we continued going hell-for-leather, enjoying the life of pre-war London, with the difference that now we had become strangers. We moved from de Walden Street to the top floor of Cheyne House, a high circular building looking down Cheyne Walk and over the river. The rent was £207 a year; for this we were provided with an enormous drawing-room, a dining-room, a bedroom with small dressing-room, a day and night nursery and, off the kitchen, accommodation for a maid and undernurse (Nanny wasn't going to clean the pram, oh no!). The baby, when he or she arrived, would share with Nanny. We didn't think it as grand as other houses, although Lord Russell of Liverpool lived on the floor beneath us; we had to walk up two flights of stairs.

In the January or February before the child was due, when I was about five months pregnant, I was dressing to go out to dinner and Robin was stretched out on the bed smoking and reading *The Times*. I happened for a moment to be gazing at my favourite view up and across the Thames; my passion is to be near water. This should have been our moment to be happy. In the eye of any beholder it must have looked so: surely we had everything going for us?

Robin, who had been out a lot recently, mostly playing bridge at the St James's Club, put down the newspaper.

'You do know,' he told me, 'that I have no intention of being faithful to you.'

I was upset, but the silence of the river helped me to know that whatever Robin did, scenes would be futile, noise was never going to touch him, that he was going to do what he was going to do and anything other than acceptance would be a waste of energy. Of course he was young and greatly influenced by his licentious father, who thought nothing of such behaviour. The violent reaction I felt inside was not physical jealousy, but more of a feeling of mental anguish because since we were eighteen, we had, as I thought, enjoyed a really extraordinary friendship. We had an amused, private relationship in which we had never found each other boring for a moment; suddenly I felt terror and anxiety that this precious part of my life was going elsewhere.

I caught sight of Robin's face in the mirror; he had on his steely look, the one that amused me when he turned it on other people, but now it was my turn. He made his announcement looking hard at me, then picked up *The Times* and continued to read.

'Explain.'

He put the paper down again.

'It won't matter at all. I think that every man ought to be honest. Men are by nature polygamous, and it isn't my temperament to be faithful. I shall sleep with whom I want, and when I want.'

I can remember my pain and fury, but I controlled all reaction and started again to comb my hair: it crossed my mind that two could play at this game.

Perhaps I should have let him know that I minded, perhaps I should have made a big scene – was that what he wanted? I shall never know because I never entirely showed my feelings to him. Somewhere inside me, perhaps, by being the daughter of Glitters and Freddy Lonsdale, I had been prepared for some such eventuality. I thought again of my mother's remarks about men.

Robin kept to his word. This was only the beginning of his double life and soon it became impossible for him to have an affair unless I knew and was upset. If ever I controlled myself to the extent of hiding my knowledge, he would somehow contrive – with a letter torn up in a wastepaper basket, with a telephone call or a visit of some kind – to make me find out. He and his mistresses would develop a code way of carrying on, and it was never any good unless I was upset – he forced me to know. At this early stage in our married lives, I was frightened, depressed, and intensely lonely. I wondered whether the thought of a child could have made him jealous. His quietness at times when he was under any form of stress was something I learned to accept; he and I never again in our lives talked at any length.

*

It soon emerged, as my time grew nearer, that Robin was having an affair with the flighty wife of one of his bridge-playing friends; they lived in a house north of the Park and Robin had known the husband since school. She was a tiny, naughty, jetset tart - totally promiscuous, fun – and she appealed to Robin's vanity.

Unlike me, the wife's husband was used to her behaviour and knew her infatuations never lasted; and anyway, he liked Robin and had no wish to quarrel.

Edward was born at Cheyne House on 13 April 1937; the birth was long, drawn-out and difficult, and by the end of it I was very tired. Robin had disappeared completely, so my mother was constantly in attendance. At the end, in misery and self-pity, I explained where he could be found – at his girlfriend's house north of the Park. As can be imagined, there was an element in Glitters' reaction of satisfaction at my desertion: now I was in the same plight as she had once been in. She could have said, 'Oh don't be silly, it's always how men behave when their wives are pregnant,' but instead she dramatized my tears, delivered her 'All men are swine' monologue, culminating in how she could not bear to see her daughter unhappy. Hilda, on the other hand, had no interest at all in Edward's birth; she never came to see her first grandchild.

At birth Edward weighed six and a half pounds and looked dead white. Robin appeared at last when summoned, not looking at all pleased and not in the least interested in the baby, though, as usual, absorbing my mother's mischievous remarks with tolerance. He then disappeared for a second time, and I was left in charge of the maternity nurse.

During his second day Edward looked even more pale and quiet than on his first; it was my mother's sense of alarm which saved the day – and his life – for she was the first to notice that he was coughing up over his pillow small quantities of blood. At first no one paid much attention to her, for the maternity nurse was in control, and nobody did anything until she gave the word; she reiterated that everything was fine. Fortunately my mother went on repeating, 'The pillow is stained with fresh crimson blood,' and, finally, as a concession to the poor woman's hysteria, a doctor was sent for. He diagnosed at once that Edward had an internal haemorrhage. Very little was understood then about this condition except that it was likely to cause death unless the child could be given a blood transfusion. There were no blood banks and the linking of groups was a more or less fortuitous business: they took blood from a relative and hoped it would work.

At that moment Robin sauntered into the flat to change for dinner and as soon as he was told of the situation, there was my good friend back again, cooperative and calm, allowing his blood to be transfused to save the baby's life. So, after hours of further anxiety, Edward recovered, and his mother and father were at last able to have dinner together again.

A few weeks later Edward gave us a further shock. He had just been circumcised. I had not been altogether in favour of the circumcision, for it was not performed for a specifically religious reason but because it was considered medically sensible to circumcise male children. As usual, I had kept my thoughts to myself but if I had voiced my doubts perhaps a second set-back in Edward's life could have been avoided.

The doctor had come in the morning and done what he assured us was necessary; Edward was left hygienically bandaged but screaming as if the world would end. My own tears seemed to be rather the accepted pattern; young mothers were treated in general as being foolish and feeble. I fitted the bill very well. Mothers in our world of 1937 had very little to do with their children, fathers absolutely nothing. I was told by the bossy maternity nurse, due to stay with us exactly a month, to pull myself together and go out and do some shopping. Sister was in charge, and Sister knew best about everything.

I did as I was told but on my return I learned that Sister had rather let the side down, for she had chosen that afternoon to invite her admirer to tea. I had not been told of this, the reason why, of course, she was so keen for me to go and indulge myself in Harrods. The object of her affection was being entertained in my drawing-room to cucumber sandwiches and plum cake which Sister had ordered our dotty Welsh maid, Gertie, to serve, and so she never heard the screams of her new-born charge.

Gertie did hear them and thought she should go and look at the baby. Edward had kicked hard enough to dislodge his dressing and had started seriously bleeding again. Gertie was a life-saver; she could not get hold of me but she telephoned Robin at his office. He arrived at Cheyne House before I did and contacted our beloved family doctor, Geoffrey Hale. When I arrived back I was met by him and an eminent paediatrician, a hysterical Sister full of plum cake, Robin and a baby that looked little better than a grey-white corpse.

Edward had lost fluid and again there was blood everywhere, so we were into a second transfusion emergency, and for a second time Robin was the hero of the hour.

I sacked Sister then and there and sent for Nanny Dawson who had been due, anyway, to appear in a few weeks' time; fortunately, having already been engaged by us, she could come at once.

If there was a museum for nannies – as they are now a thing of the ancient past – Nanny Dawson was such a perfect example she would have been stuffed and exhibited in a position of great importance, probably in the hall as you entered. Nanny Dawson was short, with rather red cheeks, crafty brown eyes and greying hair pulled back and worn in a bun. She wore a spotless, starched white overall over her outdoor rig – grey skirt, grey stockings and white blouse. When the overall came off, a well cut grey jacket was put on and a very stiff grey hat with a flat black ribbon round it, and, I never knew why, not black but very highly polished sturdy brown walking shoes. She was wonderful at her job. Edward was hardly alive when she came to him and, with her care, he grew into a normal, healthy child. She loved him dearly and always referred to him as 'Little Lord Muck', a name that stuck for a long time.

Before she came to us Nanny had been with the Oppenheimer family in Johannesburg; we must have been a terrible come-down. Until Robin went away, Nanny ran our house and the children's lives; I gave in to her over everything. The first thing she had demanded was an under-nurse to look after the Rolls Royce of prams which came from Milsom's in Wigmore Street. It was dark blue and demanded I live up to my reputation for extravagance. I bought the finest pillows and linen from Debenhams and Freebody's, Milsom's already having supplied, at great cost, an ermine rug for winter and one in fine wool for summer monogrammed for Edward in hand stitching: E.C.M.F. – Edward Charles Morice Fox.

Nanny saw this pram every day when the under-nurse, having cleaned, polished and prepared it, took it from the cellar to the front door of Cheyne House. She then walked up to our door to collect the baby, bringing him downstairs with Nanny saying 'Don't drop 'im, don't drop 'im' to put him in the pram and cover him over carefully, with Nanny glaring to see that she had done it properly. The under-nurse then retreated backwards, up the steps under Nanny's admonition: 'And you 'ave tea ready for us, the bread and butter cut thin, for when we get back, and put out some honey, jam and marmite, 'is sponge fingers and 'ave the kettle boilin'. I'm exhausted already.' Nanny and baby would then move off at a great pelt, destination Daisy Walk in Hyde Park, where she would meet all the other nannies from much grander houses than ours, there to pass the time gossiping steadily about the perfectly dreadful people who employed them and paid their wages.

I was terrified of Nanny Dawson because I had absolutely no intention of looking after the child myself and consequently did not want to lose her. My mother said I was an idiot and she was right: I remember before going out to dinner with Robin I would oversee the arrangements for Nanny's dinner. A typical menu would be a little piece of salmon, if in season, with mayonnaise; followed by English lamb, new potatoes and peas; and perhaps a lemon soufflé, or anything else she said she fancied. Nanny's great weakness was drink, specifically Guinness. It was Guinness for elevenses, Guinness for lunch, Guinness for dinner and certainly one or more for a nightcap – the dregs of the bottle were always handed to Edward. I spent a fortune on Edward's clothes at Rowe's in Bond Street and it used to surprise our guests to see a very small, angelic child attired in pale blue crêpe-de-chine suits, real silk socks and white buckskin shoes tottering round the flat swigging Guinness out of a bottle. Perhaps this early training did some good, as Edward now drinks less than anyone I know.

*

For the next two years, the Robin Foxes, as well as spending quite ordinary, conventional times with their families, continued to enjoy the social round. We were fortunate in our friends; today I never feel tempted to go to the Derby or Ascot or Goodwood or Wimbledon, because we were able to do all these things in great style. You could say we were thoroughly spoiled. We would dine at the Savoy, either in the restaurant or the Grill Room, several times a week. We went to Paris often to see Willie and he probably paid our fare; and we would go to Auteuil and Longchamps with him, and then on to Deauville for the racing there and, in winter, we would go to the Carlton Hotel at Cannes with the Marks & Spencer family. We were often guests, but we made a point of returning hospitality, so we must have been better off than I remember, or had enough security for the manager of Hoare's Bank not to have a nervous breakdown at the sight of our overdraft. But 1939 was looming and the balloon was about to go up on this way of life, for us and for everyone else.

At home my own family were around constantly. Robin thought my sisters very silly but he had moments of liking them; he had a sort of gentle contempt for the whole world and the only exceptions were those who, in the future, became his protégés. Then, the more impossible they were the more he loved them. Robin's brother and sisters, of course, never came to Cheyne House as Hilda's rage had not yet abated, and they would never have dared to come and see me without her approval.

We still continued to see the Sieffs. Uncle Simon (Marks) was a quiet, tiny, tough tycoon with huge, sad eyes; a realist, he was as hard as nails but, I believe, capable of love. He and Miriam, his wife, gave us comfort and understanding on more than one occasion; it wouldn't be an exaggeration to say that his was the biggest influence on our lives, especially in the difficult period immediately after the war.

Israel Sieff, Miriam's brother and Simon's partner, was more the showman of the outfit: fairly tall, with a great dome of a head, he was by far the most clever man I have met although not always, in his private life, the wisest or the most discreet. With his amazing blue eyes and a quizzical smile, he exerted great charm; but I have, on occasion, seen that smile vanish – and then it was time to jump to attention. I learned that he was far harder than Simon – something not easy to achieve. I intend no note of complaint by saying that both these great men were tough, for although I belonged to their children's generation I found myself very much on their wavelength, often exchanging friendly and amused glances with them. Even now, when I have to make decisions, I spend a long time thinking, 'What would Simon advise me to do?'

We also continued to visit Howard Jay Gould at Mongewell Park, sometimes still with Hilda. The lady in Howard's life still dearest to him as well as to us was Doris Keane, and we spent two Christmases at her flat overlooking Hyde Park. The walk into her drawing-room was between two white trees; there were eighteen of us for dinner, six at each table, which were laid with white linen, Georgian silver and glass, and silver candlesticks with red candles, each table crossed and re-crossed with dark red and green ribbons. After the traditional Anglo-American dinner, the lights were turned down and the curtains across the huge windows overlooking the Park were suddenly drawn: there stood a great tree with hundreds of lighted candles fluttering. We gasped with surprise like children. We gasped even more when each of us got the presents he or she longed for from the tree.

Willie came to visit us at Cheyne Walk when he was in London. He introduced us to his friend, Lady Furness, who had been the Prince of Wales's mistress until Wallis Simpson had taken her place. An American too, she was the twin sister of Gloria

Vanderbilt and longed to be in America with her sister, but she stayed in England because she remained married to Lord Furness, a shipping magnate, and they had a little boy.

Thelma Furness was a handsome, elegant woman who wore beautiful black pearls renowned for their value; they suited her to perfection. Her clothes were French, and of great simplicity; with her very dark hair parted in the middle and worn in the nape of her neck, and her white, sad, sensual face, she had immense style – her style. She copied no one. Thelma belonged to a café society set of very versatile and experienced women – 'poules de luxe' they might be called – plentiful enough in that period, who took the Royal Wish as a command. It had been accepted that if the Prince of Wales fancied a lady she became his mistress that evening.

Although Thelma was older than we were, she grew fond of Robin and me and for a while we made a threesome. She never complained of how odiously she had been treated. She spoke only once of Wallis Simpson: we had been to a cinema and were eating smoked salmon by the fire – she did not care for restaurants. Robin opened some champagne and she quietly told the two of us what a great friend of hers Wallis had been, and how it had been she who had introduced Wallis to the future King of England. One day Thelma had heard that her beloved sister, Gloria, was ill in New York, and felt impelled to go and stay with her for a few days. She begged her best friend to take good care of the heir to the throne, and to do everything she could to make him happy. As history relates, her wish was granted.

A new friend I made at this time was the journalist Godfrey Winn; we met him first weekending at Howard Gould's house, where he had been invited for his prowess at tennis and bridge. Godfrey had once wanted, he let us know, to be a serious novelist, but Somerset Maugham had advised him that he would never be in the first division. In Maugham's opinion, Godfrey had the makings of a successful journalist, and this is what he became – the highest paid writer in the land. Later he wrote a lot of books about himself which became bestsellers. He was a tough man in his dealings but mercurial in temperament. If we were in favour, his books were sent inscribed to us, but if we were out of favour, we didn't receive a copy.

I became very fond of this odd, effeminate man and was pleased and surprised that our friendship survived to his last book, *The Positive Hour* which is dedicated to Robin and me. Robin never really liked him at all, though at times he tolerated and teased him: but when, two years after Edward's birth, I was going to have another child, it was Godfrey who never once left my side. While I was pregnant his sympathetic symptoms became a joke: if I felt ill, he felt ill. The idea of the child obsessed him, and when I was about to have the baby he had to be forcibly persuaded to leave the room.

James's birth, on 19 May 1939, was plain sailing: he was born within about four hours of my coming under starter's orders, with absolutely no difficulty at all. Maybe the fact that he was born so easily is the reason why he was always a beautiful child. Even in adolescence he never went through an ugly phase. However, he was an obstinate, self-willed, rather violent baby and the task of bringing him up could well have defeated me, but it didn't defeat Nanny Dawson. Robin loathed her; I was terrified of her; but children loved her and did as they were told. We originally called James William and still do, but later in life, he adopted the name James under an Equity ruling to avoid two actors having identical names. Godfrey, of course, became his godfather: a good one, and I have often thought they were rather similar in looks.

Most reflections on the evils of war are correct but in our own immediate circle I saw some good come out of it: by good, I mean the chance for young men to break away from responsibilities imposed by mothers or wives, or by domineering tycoons who had built business empires which their offspring were being trained to inherit and administer according to rigid rules laid down by the founders. For many others, too, amid the terrors and heartache of parting, there was an opportunity to escape and at least the chance to try something else. The young, of course, had little idea of what the horrors of war entailed. Specifically, war to Robin and me spelt release from the powerful and self-indulgent figures of Willie and Hilda – the freedom to become ourselves. Whether this was ultimately a good or a bad thing no one can say, but it did lead in time to our finding a new and more challenging relationship with one another.

*

In July 1939 Robin was called up and joined the Honourable Artillery Company, so I moved the young family, plus Nanny and under-nurse and our London maids, to an expensive house in Bolney, Sussex. My feet cannot have been very near the ground, because I also took on the indoor and outdoor staff that went with the house; my mother and my sister Elizabeth came too. During my performance as country house hostess, Neville Chamberlain told us we were at war, and the sirens sounded. Willie upped sticks and rushed to Portugal and then to America, leaving the Fox family finances in a parlous state: he had run through the vast fortune left him by his father, Samson. On the credit side, however, at the outbreak of war all personal quarrels between myself and Hilda were put aside, at least for the war's duration, and little Edward became 'A Bird of Love Divine', a term she used for all small children. As for my own father, Freddy, he, like Willie, fled to the States with one of his lovely young ladies; but he did leave Leslie enough money to live on.

None of this, however, helped my own financial situation: Simmonds and Simmonds did not lose a moment before announcing that Robin's salary would cease altogether, and I was broke, with a number of responsibilities that had to be met. Godfrey Winn had a legendary reputation for being mean, yet he was the only person who cared enough to recognize my plight. I never even had to mention it to him, he intuitively knew, and lent me enough money to rent a cottage in the centre of Cuckfield in Sussex, a large village some fifteen miles north of Brighton.

So with his help I moved the family to Ockenden Cottage. How we stayed the course in the next five years of war I shall never quite know; it was a precarious existence at the best of times.

During the early phase of the war Robin and I did see each other occasionally: he would come to the cottage on a motor bike from Essex where he was stationed whenever he got forty-eight hours' leave, which was fairly often. In the beginning they made him a lance-bombardier, but pretty fast they moved him on to being a full bombardier. One of my greatest shocks was to see him on one of these leaves when the HAC transferred him to being a dogsbody in the Royal Artillery. He had now joined an anti-aircraft regiment and his entrance in this new role caused gales of laughter. We had last seen him as an elegant young-man-about town; what arrived now was a dirty, dishevelled bombardier in hobnailed boots, ill-cut khaki trousers and jacket made of very coarse cloth, with a forage cap perched on his head which in no way disguised the worst pudding-basin haircut of all time. A bath, a change of clothes and a good breakfast did a lot to restore his spirits, but we all considered his appearance a disappointment – these things were still absurdly important.

At another time Robin and I found ourselves temporarily in unforgettably uncomfortable lodgings at Loughton, where Robin's unit was in charge of an anti-aircraft gun. It would not have been the faintest use if the Germans had arrived, as none of them understood how to work it, nor were they supplied with ammunition. However, the squalor, bitter cold and painful discomfort taught us both endurance.

During the same period Godfrey Winn was in France as a journalist, experiencing very different conditions: he stayed at the Ritz in Paris, and dined at GHQ with the General. He was being treated, he told me, like a cabinet minister. He wrote me carefree letters bubbling with gaiety:

> My life is brimming over – and I really feel something is
> happening at last – It is like a dream – I can't really believe
> I am here and that things are really as they seem – How

My mother 'Glitters'

So rich and so lonely: Willie Fox

The paternal playwright
Freddie

His grandson the jackal

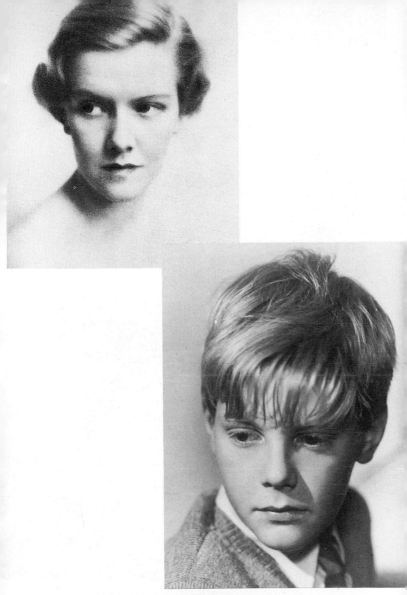

Like mother like son...me and James
(in 'The Magnet')

Marcus Sieff and Robin by the Sea of Galilee

Gladys Cooper, this time stealing Robert

much I shall have to tell you when I return – I hope to be back in a fortnight, or so – as I have to report to Bevin at the War Office – Then I hope I shall be allowed to go off on a warship somewhere, to write about that. But the only thing to do is to take each day as it comes – I am frightfully well and adoring every minute – I can't tell you how v helpful all the really big people have been – I expected so much red tape and blank minds – instead everyone talks the same language, our language.

Robin's next move was to Shrivenham in Wiltshire, where he was turned into an artillery lieutenant: his very good black hair grew with alacrity, and it seemed that overnight he was transformed into an elegant officer. But the going at Shrivenham was pretty rough, too. I remember staying with friends near the camp and Robin turned up late because his boots had been frozen to the floor.

From Shrivenham he was posted to Scotland, to Dundee, to join another anti-aircraft regiment, and here began a happy stay. He liked his colonel and the second-in-command at once and it was not long before he was Captain Fox, the adjutant. He became almost as Scottish as Burns, whose 'Ode to the Haggis' he rendered accurately and with immense drama, on every possible occasion; he was much loved by his company. Then something worse than a bomb fell on him: his colonel was retired and a young man from Liverpool, called John Turner, was posted in to take his place.

Robin's sadness and anger knew no bounds; there was a great deal of talk about how he was going to make this man's life a living hell and the early weeks, even months, were difficult. But war could draw strangers together in the most uncanny way. John Turner and Robin served together until 1945; they formed a very close relationship, which only ended when John died, about a year before Robin.

Before Robin went abroad, however, there were several periods of seven-day leaves; we spent these in London at the

Dorchester with Michael and Daphne Sieff. Michael had started the war in possession of a motorbike and the idea that he was in the Fire Brigade, but in no time he landed in the Royal Army Ordnance Corps with a high rank – I can only remember him as a full colonel. As a skilled retailer of merchandise, the contribution he could make to Ordnance was invaluable, so he never did ordinary military chores like fighting, to which anyway he would not have been suited. He became the perfect square peg in a square hole, liked and respected by everyone for whom and with whom he worked.

Our seven-day leaves were luxurious fun, with parties every night. Spirits remained high while everyone prepared for they knew not what; the bombs had not yet begun to fall, but when they did Godfrey was there to report them. Then Robin, John Turner and many thousands of other soldiers left for North Africa in 1941. Robin and I said goodbye, and I never heard his voice again, even on the telephone, until 1945.

5

Canadians in Cuckfield

It was a world of women and babies. My youngest sister, Yvonne, also came to live at Ockenden Cottage with me; her first husband was a regular soldier who had been posted to Burma. What with Nanny and Glitters on the scene, it was hard to maintain some sort of equilibrium in the household. My mother told us flatly that although war had broken out, standards must be maintained, and the silver kept safe and spotless. As it was now my silver I could have answered quite sharply, but mother's influence was still strong, so with a lot of giggling my sisters and I took the silver to a shed in the garden. The shed looked like an air-raid shelter and it probably was safer there. Bombing had started in London, and we now heard every day the steady throb of German planes en route for the city. But Nanny Dawson stormed in and told us she could not work for ill-bred Women who were Frightened of the Germans. I lost my temper and almost sacked her. Then I realized what a state of insecurity and anxiety I was really in. Suddenly I could no longer bear wondering how I was going to pay to keep family and home running.

I shook for days, knowing I must tell Nanny that the time for our parting had come. When finally I found the courage to do so, I told her the truth: I hadn't got enough money for her wages. She replied, 'I know that. I won't take no money anyway. I shall stay and look after my boys and run this place for you: you'll never do it on your own.' The latter part of her statement wasn't true; I did learn quite quickly how to run the house but in return for her generosity, Nanny wanted to be the boss of absolutely everything to do with all our lives. A little while later, when my gratitude to this old warhorse was tried to the limits, I found the guts to tell her that she must go: she was growing into an old lady now, and she went to live in Bath where her sister and brother-in-law were running a chemist's shop. The time had come for me to be head cook and bottlewasher – and mother – to my own children.

I was still in close touch with Godfrey, who had now returned from France. He put his name down for the RAF (though he was two years over age) but failed his maths exam the first time and had to retake it. While waiting for his call-up papers he was despatched by the Air Ministry to Yorkshire to write an article on the first bombing raid on Berlin; another Fleet Street scoop for Godfrey Winn. He was then sent by the *Sunday Express* to write on the horrors of the East End blitz:

> I think the page would have made history. It never appeared because at six o'clock on Friday night, Robertson sent for Gordon and killed it, because indirectly it attacked the government, and he had promised Beaverbrook that not one word of criticism of the Government should appear. Yet it was Beaverbrook himself who once urged me to speak and write for the common people. You will be the saviour of the submerged classes, he said.

Later Godfrey wrote another piece, which was published. This time he stayed up every night of the week:

> The ARP posts were in Finsbury, where in one place there was a direct hit on a First Aid Post, and yet the wounded nurses, within ten minutes, had a room set up with blankets over the shattered windows, one hurricane lamp, attending to the wounded from outside. And the hospital I described was St Mary's at Paddington. We had an incredible night.

The patients never murmured, the surgeons never became flustered, as for myself, the only time I felt for a moment things were getting on top of me was when I had to wheel a dead policeman into the mortuary. His mate, who had brought him from Edgware Road, kept on saying over and over again: he has the bed next to me in the station house. He had been hit by blast, his nose was plugged with blood from the internal haemorrhage, his eyes were still open, the wave in his fair hair looked so young, you kept on wondering what had happened to his helmet, it was so strange to see a policeman lying down, without his helmet. Hours later, I drove home, through the fires, and in Edgware Road, a policeman stopped me, and politely explained the route to Victoria in the new terms of shattered streets. His voice was quiet and polite and unruffled. But I recognized his voice in the darkness as the voice that had kept on saying, he has the bed next to me in the station house . . .

Godfrey went on to complain, however, that really

The worst nightmare – even worse than the greedy triumphant fires, the ones in Carlton House Terrace the other night that made the whole Mall a molten hell with reflections on the windows of Buck House like hundreds of scarlet eyes peering out at the crazy madness – the worst nightmare is no longer seeing one's friends.

My own worse nightmare, with capable Nanny gone and Violet my cook, was being faced with something called an Ideal Boiler. 'Ideal for whom?' I asked, as I kicked the bloody thing which, under my administration, had gone out for what seemed like the hundredth time. But gradually boilers were conquered, children were organized, Elizabeth was married off to the strange man of her dreams, Carnegie (Kinny) Pawson, a sporting amateur who once won the Scottish Grand National. And we got round the authorities to let Yvonne off National Service so that she could stay and help me. I even summoned up the courage to inform the paying guests I had taken into the house to make ends meet that they should depart. The money might have helped, but mutual loathing rather took the edge off things.

There was, however, one more paying guest who arrived soon after that. Leslie Lonsdale – she had been alone in her house in London and we no longer knew what had happened to her daughters. They may have been generous and helped their mother with money, even with letters and telephone calls, but if they did she never told us. It was at Glitters' suggestion that she came to us; I quite understood that my mother needed the companionship of someone of her own generation.

Immaculate, amusing, full of charm, but bone idle, Lesley informed me one day that her greatest joy would be to have an open fire in her bedroom. I must have been very weak or distracted with worry, but I did the grate for her so that this whim could be satisfied. I confess she was such good value that I ended up sitting on the floor laughing at myself with her. Still, although Leslie paid me four pounds a week, there was no way that this honeymoon could last. I grew more and more harassed over lack of funds and too much to do and as a result I grew more and more irritable.

My mother finally, though with great difficulty, realized that the Foxes were not giving the family one penny; with her own generous nature, this was hard for her to accept for she knew, as I did, that they were still comfortably off. She and Leslie found a cottage they could share, at Charlwood, near Reigate. The fact that they had no transport, and would consequently be isolated, seemed to have escaped their notice, as did the fact that while they were still out of London they now lay on the direct route of the German bombers to the capital, who often dropped their odious cargo on the way back if they had failed to find a target. I think of these two women, whatever their faults, as an example of perfect friendship. Now that they were verging on old age – which must have surprised them – they were still defiant and courageous, and put up with the bombs and the sleepless nights with an arrogant disregard for peril.

*

Attitudes were changed totally by war. When the death of one of my friends is announced today, I am appalled and shattered. I wonder if, in times of horror, there is not some force that protects us from the full impact of loss. At that time, while I do not believe we were hard-hearted, so many of those we loved and were closest to were here today and gone tomorrow that we took it in our stride.

People will not tell the truth about the war, but women left behind like myself naturally formed attachments. My first of these was to an Englishman, a twenty-seven year old captain in the 8th Army who was stationed in Cuckfield for a time. I saw him walking through the village one day and thought, with surprise, 'Now there's an attractive man.' I used to go to Bexhill to meet him, but for security reasons I was turned back – the Germans were expected to invade. At another time I had a French friend who was parachuted into France and brought me back Vogue and scent.

When the Canadians arrived and took over south-east England I was ready, perhaps, for more serious friendships. Canadian Corps Headquarters was at Wakehurst Place, several miles from Ockenden Cottage, which was on the main road, and I used to see handsome men being driven past our door in smart cars with flags fluttering on the bonnet. I also noticed that they had red tabs on their uniforms: I knew little of army protocol, but it took me no time to learn that these passengers were at least full colonels or brigadiers, which meant they had power and authority.

Yvonne and I also learned that they gave good parties every weekend although we, as civilians, had no cars or transport and therefore little chance of getting to Headquarters and back, even if invited. However, we soon made friends and our anxieties were more than offset by the gaiety that came into our lives with these charming strangers. I cannot claim I behaved very well and I don't intend to dwell on that, but I am proud of the friendships we established.

I soon became attached to one of these officers, whom I shall call Mark. When I first met him he had been pointed out to me as an uncommunicative brute. I went over.

'You look very surly and miserable,' I said.

'I *am* surly and miserable.'

I was flattered by his subsequent attentions. I'm not sure that I really liked him, but it is very important to be needed, and while he was rich, decisive, had a high opinion of himself – and seemed unattainable – he was more in need of friendship than most of us. To be frank, he could also be a bit of a bore but I liked being part of his world.

Edward and James had many friends of their own and accepted the fact that the house was always full of Canadians or Americans, sometimes English or Frenchmen, who came in to have a meal with my sister and me. If we were interested in one man more than another, I don't think they had the faintest idea. The Canadians, particularly, enjoyed the company of children. I can remember Mark arranging to take them in the woods near Cuckfield Park, and telling them he wanted them to listen very carefully because some Red Indians were going to find us: there would be a prize for the first one who heard them coming. It was autumn and the ground was covered with dry leaves. We waited for about a quarter of an hour. Everything was absolutely still then suddenly, out of the trees appeared three men in battledress close enough to touch. The experience was most enjoyable, even for grown-ups. I asked them to go away two or three hundred yards and come towards us again, expecting this time we would see them. I was wrong. The men were descended from Red Indians and attached to one of the regiments under Mark's command.

I would not have tolerated anyone who made the children

unhappy, and if any liaison caused scenes, then it would finish that second. It was all very civilized, but I did not want marriages broken up. I can remember explaining, 'English women are very tough: if we say goodbye, we say goodbye.' Then there would be the sound of a car revving up, accompanied by the smell of petrol. Our lives were controlled by transport.

As well as being very busy, Mark liked to visit the headquarters of his regiments when they had parties, and this was pretty nearly every weekend. I suppose this entertaining was to keep up morale while the men hung about training and waiting to invade France. Spirits were very high, there was always a good band and, being Canadians, no shortage of food or drink. I think I was a help to Mark because I enjoyed going with him and could always remember names and prompt him: although he was an able man, this was one thing he found very difficult.

We went all over southern England together. I must have had more courage then than I have now. I remember approaching Portsmouth to attend some regimental gathering, and the nearer his driver got the more we could see the city was being heavily bombed. Very laconically, Mark said we had better go on, and go on we did. In fact, we drove straight into an air raid when any sane human being would have turned and fled. The regimental headquarters was not touched but it took ages to reach and we passed through scenes of terrible fire and devastation. Because Mark was a general my presence was accepted without comment, though normally civilians were not allowed near the coast.

For a change we went for weekends to Elaine Blond, the youngest sister of Simon Marks, who kept a huge house at East Grinstead. It was called Saint Hill and she ran her house as if there was no war on, although the sight of men in uniform everywhere contradicted this.

Elaine's main interests in life were the Queen Victoria Hospital at East Grinstead and her friendship with the great plastic surgeon there, Archibald McIndoe. The hospital was the main centre in England for plastic surgery, receiving vast support from

Canada and from Elaine, her husband and family. The Queen Mother is now the patron.

It was the delicacy of Archie's work which was so impressive, restoring faces, hands and bodies, whenever possible, of young men hideously injured in war. One day I asked if he had always been such an outstanding surgeon. 'A good, competent surgeon, experienced, yes,' he replied, 'but when I looked at a burned boy for the first time and saw that I must replace his eyelids, God came down my right arm.' This from a tough, extrovert New Zealander with strong, spatulate fingers is something I shall never forget. There are only twenty-four hours in a day but I felt Archie doubled their number. He not only performed many operations but always found time to know his patients well enough to explain what had to be done, however horrendous, and why, and he would never start until they had understood and could co-operate with him.

I heard many instances of this, and often met the men concerned. Archie and his welfare officer, Blackie Blackwell, thought it important to have lively and attractive girls around the patients when they were starting to recover from their operations. These girls had to show no signs of horror or of shock, even revulsion, they felt on looking at these men for the first time. I was often around and fitted into this category: I hope I never grew thick-skinned, but I learnt quickly to disguise the effect the sight of these appalling injuries, on men little older than schoolboys, had on me.

If ever there was too much pity or bathos, Archie would tell us not to be sorry now, but to remember these men in forty years' time, when they were no longer heroes and when no one would either know or care what became of them.

There was one very sad case I remember in particular. A young man had been shot down at sea and had managed to blow up the rubber boat that they carried, but he had been so many days on the water alone that not only was he starving, but his feet were badly frost-bitten. Thirst had been about to kill him when he had managed to snatch at a gull that landed on his rubber boat, and wrung its neck – the blood saved his life. Soon afterwards he was seen, picked up and taken to the Queen Victoria Hospital, East Grinstead. Skilful treatment restored him to life but finally, after every effort had been made, Archie had to tell him that he must amputate the legs below the knee. The young man's response was one not often encountered – in no circumstances would he submit. Archie saw him every day and explained again and again what he had to do. Finally the boy gave way, and the operation took place. When he was recovering and having artificial limbs fitted, he showed great courage, largely because he had fallen in love with one of the nurses, to whom he became engaged and soon married. After the wedding they went for a slap-up meal in a restaurant with friends and ordered roast chicken; a bone stuck in his throat, and he choked on it and died.

The boys and I shared a warm friendship with Felicity 'Flick' Fairfax-Ross, married to a brigadier who was away; she had three children. Flick was like an original of *To the Manor Born*, with a large house near the village where she kept first-class staff too old to be called up. She was beautiful in an outdoors way, autocratic, spoiled, but courageous – a woman who lived for hunting and ski-ing. She also was an expert at breeding labradors, which she trained as gun dogs.

Flick was conventional and bossy and in one other way perfectly normal: she was vain, and adored the admiration of the Canadians who, quite rightly, thought she was 'the greatest'. She rather disapproved of me at first and it took me quite a time to realize this: she was cross, even rather jealous, because while I appeared to get other people to do things for me, she had to take on the world single-handed. Of course, this was nonsense. We both went exactly our own ways, yet we were equally capable of getting help and assistance when we wanted it. The standards she maintained took a great deal of effort on her part, and were important in forming the character values of her own children – and mine – when war was generally making social life very lack-lustre.

Flick always had Christopher Stone, her step-father, to stay at Christmas. He was the first really well-known personality in the world of gramophone records, and introduced his own programme on the wireless. The seasonal ball was set rolling by Flick's tea party, where about twenty of us would sit down to a traditional bun fight: toast and scones, bread and butter, different home-made jams and honey, sponge cakes for the little ones, and an enormous cake in the middle of the table with wonderful icing and candles – the candles because it was also Flick's birthday, so every child brought a present. Even the crackers, pulled after tea, were full of lovely things. If Tommy, her husband, was home, he would appear as Father Christmas, bringing a present for every child. When war took him away we found understudies, chosen from members of the Canadian Army Medical Corps who were at the hospital a hundred yards down the road. After the huge tea, we had games – charades, hunt the slipper, postman's knock, musical chairs. As the clock started ticking towards bedtime, there would be oranges and lemons and the final fling – Sir Roger de Coverly. Flick taught Edward and James how to ride and fish, how to handle a gun and enjoy rough shooting; she also taught them how to behave – or rather how not to behave – with other people's dogs. With their father away, the boys were lucky to learn the finer points about country life so young.

*

While wife and children were thus occupied, Robin was with the First Army in North Africa, with war pulling him slowly towards Italy. We should have been in touch through something called a joint account at the bank, if for no other reason, but soon this contact came to an end – he had spent whatever was in it. I don't blame him. He communicated sometimes in letters which were finely written, almost poetic, but rather impersonal. He would describe, for example, the agony, even the beauty of war. It is difficult for me to say anything about Robin's war because when he did finally come home, the first thing he insisted on was that the subject was never – but never – to be mentioned. Some years later I learned that he had landed near Sorrento; we were in Sorrento at the time and had to leave a restaurant because the bullet marks on the walls disturbed him too much. Usually, he was unmoved by emotion, indeed notorious for being so.

I do know that at some stage he left the Artillery to command a radar unit, becoming one of the first officers to hold such a job; and that at another time, probably as liaison officer, he joined the Poles, who awarded him the Virtuti Militari, the Polish equivalent of the VC. He won the Military Cross, awarded on the completion of a mission during which he would not take cover or receive help for injuries. He had been with his commanding officer, John Turner, and they were caught in an ambush: John was driving like hell while Robin was returning the fire and killed at least one German. He was hit in the back and missed death by a hair, while another bullet made a hole through his beret (I still have the beret).

When he was taken to hospital there seemed little hope: the bullet had grazed his lung, causing serious infection. One night, a certain Philip Evans, colonel in charge of the hospital, was sitting at his desk very depressed because he did not have enough of the new drug, penicillin, to save more than the lives of a few of the soldiers in his care. Wearily, by the light of a torch, he looked down the names and particulars of the injured, and the name Cuckfield caught his eye. Now his wife and sons lived in Cuckfield – by such a thread can life hang – and so Philip Evans sought out my husband's bed, perceived for certain that he was dying, and gave him some of his last remaining antibiotic. Robin lived and wrote to tell me of this, saying there was little he could do in return but that he felt unbelievably grateful, so would I try to do something for Philip Evans's wife.

I mounted my bicycle as I knew where she lived: her name was Dr Barbara Evans and I knew her by sight as pathologist to Archie McIndoe. I set out up the hill to her house. She was tall, red-headed, rather frightening and aloof. I took courage into my hands, apologized for appearing unannounced and thanked her profusely. What could I do for her, I asked. She looked at me with disdain.

'The only thing I want is not possible.'

'May I ask what could that be?'

'A bottle of Lanvin's Arpège scent.' By this time I was really disliking her.

'Well, that's only too easy,' I was able to say.

'What do you mean?'

Positively snapping, 'Never mind,' I got on my bike, whizzed down the hill and went to my secret cupboard, well-stocked with French scent given to me by an admirer who had got it the year before in the Dieppe raid (he had brought back as much as he could stuff into his pockets, plus a DSO for himself). I seized the biggest bottle of Lanvin I could find and, after a second bicycle ride up the hill, made my presentation; at least she had the grace to laugh.

From now on I did hear news of Robin, particularly from Marcus Sieff, who was now a brigadier connected with the landing of troops and equipment in Italy. He got home to England sometimes, and told me about the fun he and Robin had had, first in North Africa and then in Italy. Rome, particularly, seemed to be a happy hunting ground – the pace of pleasure in between times of stress was fast and furious. I remember once being in the Savoy with Mark. My eye was drawn towards the top of the staircase leading into the restaurant and I saw a man in rather pale, tropical uniform: it was Marcus. In his authoritarian way he was looking at the names of people who had booked tables that evening, and he must have recognized Mark's because almost immediately he looked across and came bounding towards us. It was a wonderful, hugging reunion, and we spent the rest of the evening talking about Robin and hearing what he had been up to. Mark was paying the bill and being very good-natured the drink really started to flow. He seemed to be enjoying himself as much as we were: seeing Marcus at that moment was a great tonic, especially as I was bracing myself to face the departures of friends, inevitable but, nevertheless, painful.

When the war had finally ended and the survivors were drifting home, the business of waiting for Robin to announce the actual date of his return became irksome. One evening I accepted an invitation from the Sieffs to some high-powered party given by a South American millionaire whom I knew vaguely; it was to be at the Savoy in the room where, ten years earlier, Robin and I sat down to our wedding breakfast. As I was setting off Robin telephoned me. I did recognize his voice, just; he was not sure of the time of his arrival, so I told him where I would be.

The party was everything that had been promised. When we wanted to dance, we went from the Pinafore Room to the restaurant; it was a little like pre-war days again but I remember feeling slightly bored as I had no particular interest in any of the men. Suddenly a tall figure walked into the room, and I recall turning to the group I was sitting with, laughing and admitting to them that I knew that I wasn't on very good form. 'Now, you see that man over there, that man who has just walked into the room,' I said, 'the good-looking dark one, with that marvellous, aggressive walk. Now if he came over to the table, something tells me that I would cheer up.'

It was Marcus Sieff who replied, 'There's a very good chance that he will. It's your husband, Bob Fox.'

PART TWO

6

Services Rendered

> Your raven's eye,
> the dancing grin.
> Head held high
> and soldier's
> unastonished stride.

Dirk Bogarde's description of Robin, though written much later, was perfect for the stranger who walked into the Pinafore Room of the Savoy. Major Robin Fox, MC. His return was exactly like a dream; at that moment my previous life seemed not to exist, although Ockenden Cottage and the two children were there to prove otherwise: I had put them to bed and kissed them good-night before setting out on this unlikely evening.

When Major Fox made his entrance more champagne appeared as quick as lightning, as if the waiters had been cued in for that very moment. The warmth of the greeting he got from the Sieffs and his other friends was overwhelming. I have no idea what I was doing while the rejoicing raged around me. I think I sat there grinning and thinking how handsome and fit this man looked. A voice inside me kept repeating, 'It isn't true, it isn't true'. But it was. Finally, in the small hours, the band stopped playing the tunes to which we had danced away the last five years, the champagne seemed a little flat, goodbyes and endless arrangements for meetings were shouted on the pavement as taxis drew up in the Savoy courtyard. Robin and I were pushed into one. We were complete strangers setting out on an unknown course. In fact we had no course at all – the only reality we shared was Edward and James. Had it not been for the boys, I think he would have dropped me at Neville and Elaine Blond's flat in Arlington Street, where they had invited us to stay. He would have bade me goodnight, possibly have said it was a pleasure to meet me and then vanished forever. I had grown to expect that kind of farewell. As it was, he, the father of my children, accompanied me into the building and we got into the lift and sailed to the top floor.

There was little time for happy celebrations of his home-coming. We knew at once that we had not a penny between us. Robin, and thousands like him who had been away for four years or more, had practically nothing, along with a demob suit that was totally unwearable. Our first conversation was about money – or rather the lack of it – and there were many of these to follow. Over coffee in the morning we agreed that although he had never liked practising as a lawyer, and detested being at Simmonds and Simmonds, he must return to the firm, at least temporarily, to keep four bodies and souls together. Percy and Teddy, the twin senior partners, and Gordon, Teddy's son and Robin's contemporary and friend, received him affectionately, and told him he could come back and start work at a salary of £700 a year – the same as he had received before being called up. Astonished, Robin told them that he had been away for five years, and now had two boys getting to preparatory school age. Their answer was that after five years away from law practice, he would be stale and therefore worth less to them, not more, but they wanted to be generous because he was a personal friend of the family.

This was hard for Robin and me to take but we agreed that Robin must tell the Simmonds' what to do with their offer, and never go back, and that somehow we would manage. We stood at the window in the Blonds' flat, high above Green Park, and looked down together. Though we had little self-pity it was hard not to feel despair. We were reacting, I suspect, from very different memories of the last five years; for both of us these had been hectic and intense, and we were wondering where to go from here.

Fate – or as so often in our case, the Marks and Sieff families – was hovering close at hand. A night or two later we went round to 47 Grosvenor Square to be welcomed by Simon and Miriam Marks. Simon enquired after our circumstances and, though he said nothing to us that night, very shortly afterwards he summoned Robin to his office. 'You remember Jules Stein?' he asked.

'You mean the head of MCA?' said Robin.

'Yes.'

'I do vaguely,' replied Robin. 'I was an articled clerk, and before the war had the job of getting him his LCC licence for the firm to operate in London.'

'Well, he's back in London, with the plan of opening offices here, and he wants a young lawyer to get the business off the ground. I have suggested you as being the man for the job. He is at Claridges. Go and see him, he's expecting you.'

Robin went round at once to see the head of the Music Corporation of America – the biggest film and theatre agency in the world, known bluntly as the 'Human Octopus'. Jules Stein put him through some short, sharp questioning and engaged him as lawyer to the London office. He was to be joined by Laurence Evans, who had been general manager of the Old Vic Company in its two first famous seasons at the New Theatre, and Jules was also sending over Jimmy McHugh Jnr, son of the famous song writer, to teach them American know-how. Small offices were acquired in Dover Street, and not much later MCA London was on the map.

When Jimmy arrived to dispense American expertise he could not understand England, or Englishmen, and was soon showing visible signs of distress. Neither could he stand the nanny he and his wife had engaged to look after their child. I remember being the first one to assure 'Lol' Evans that McHugh was bonkers, and that he would soon be gone. I was right. He and his pretty wife fled to Hollywood, but not before he had set light to nanny's nightdress.

'Lol' and Robin got on well and formed the nucleus of a strong team. 'Tycoon' is the word that summed up their boss, Jules Stein. A small, dark, slim man with hair just beginning to go grey, he wore glasses, talked very little, but to the point, in a staccato manner. He was sharp, but not without humour. I liked Jules Stein and I think he liked us – as much as he was capable of liking any employee – but if for one second Robin had not proved up to the job: 'Out!' Jules was married to Doris, his exact female double. She was dressed in sables, which, with her wonderful diamonds, quite startled shabby London. He used to be kitted out by the most expensive Savile Row tailors: vicuna overcoats over perfect suits, silk shirts and ties from Sulka, always in the light-to-dark-blue range, black shoes by Tuczek. The hair was rather blue, too, and on top of it went a dark blue Homburg: surely Locke's could not sell even an American a dark blue hat?

Managing director of MCA was Lew Wasserman, tough and sinister (at least to us English), tall, dark-haired and pasty, with a cleft palate which gave him an impediment in his speech. Whenever he came to London, the pressure stepped up. MCA represented the bulk of all American stage and screen stars and with the end of the war they were drifting back to Europe, so Robin and Lol's job was to look after these terrestrial beings while they worked or played in London. There were many of them, because writers and directors and producers were also on the list. The agent's job was to put the most suitable clients into the best-paying jobs, and keep them in work. Everything was fine so long as the clients made the money ring in the box office till; if that sound grew faint: 'Out!'

*

Quite early on during his time with MCA, Robin said he wished to speak to me seriously, and I put on my straight face. I recalled that previous occasion at Cheyne House before the war when I was pregnant with Edward, and Robin had told me of his impending infidelities. He now informed me that in no circumstances was I to know or even speak to any of his clients. I knew what he meant. We had all grown up.

Outwardly I showed not the faintest sign that I was affected. Many of my friends were now telling me I was splendid, attractive, special – not that this made me take myself any more seriously than before – so I just decided to let any future infidelities on Robin's part take their course. But the prospect did somewhat take the wind out of my sails, and put paid to the pleasant and rising euphoria I had felt when Robin had first been given his glamorous job.

At this time, my mother, who had a gift for rehabilitating unfortunates, discovered a wonderful woman called Alice Stevens who, when her chauffeur-turned-gamekeeper husband died of tuberculosis, had been turned out of her cottage with her nine-year-old daughter. Walking by chance in a lane close to Cuckfield, she met my mother and told her of her plight. Glitters said I must take this woman and her daughter, Rosemary, and give them accommodation at the cottage in return for cooking and helping with the boys.

I grumbled and argued but my arguments were finally overcome and so Alice became part of the family. She was a good cook, her speciality being things like roly-poly baked jam pudding. She and Rosemary became part of the family and my children's friends seemed to live in the house too. Two of these were called Robin Edwards and Brian Rogers but for some reason known only to themselves and the boys, the four of them were known as Charles, Charles, Charles and Charles. The evenings were given up to plays, in which the Fox brothers displayed a singular lack of talent. Their joy in life was expressed through football and secondhand bikes. Rosemary was treated like a sister as well as being a big help to me.

Alice, at first, had an overpowering admirer called Sergeant Fly, whom the boys always referred to as 'Fly in the Ointment'.

Having watched him assist Rosemary with her handstands on the lawn, I remember feeling that I should have to steel myself to manoeuvre his departure from our circle. I needn't have worried, for Alice then assured me she was going to marry him. She was consequently as surprised as I was relieved when he announced that he must return to his missus. Alice was disconsolate but I told her I was psychic and could see a small, fair man about to come into her life, and that he could spell happiness. Fiercely she assured me that she hated small, fair men, but when a small fair one did turn up, known as Sidney Mitchell, they were at the altar in a flash.

Robin always rather disliked Ockenden Cottage: although large by cottage standards and attractively low-ceilinged with medieval beams, it was hardly in the style to which he had been accustomed as a child. He had been brought up in what he called 'real country' – Yorkshire – and in great houses like Bolton Abbey. At Ockenden, there was about half an acre of garden which I loved and with which Elizabeth had helped me. Both of us had worked immensely hard, turning it from the village rubbish dump into a very pretty and much admired cottage garden. Robin was not faintly interested in all this. He felt that Cuckfield was suburbia. The cottage was attached to an old-fashioned bakery which later we bought and converted; there was always the smell of yeast, which visitors loved and Robin hated. He tried commuting daily to London but that lasted no time at all, so he arranged to stay during the week with his sister, Pamela, in Kensington. Pamela was happily married to a gentle intellectual called Maurice Michael, a literary agent; they had a little girl and a spare room. Robin returned home at the weekend: this habit was lifelong and unbroken. No glamorous actress could break the pattern, but some mistresses were invited quite regularly to spend Sunday with us; in fact the oftener any of them was invited, the more it became clear that the power of her charms was on the wane. I would then begin, in imagination, to conjure up a successor. I never had to wait long.

There was one side of this odd set-up, however, which was

perfect: where Robin and the two boys were concerned there was complete harmony and understanding. There is no doubt that he loved Edward and James deeply but he could not express this easily to them. He never scolded or criticized them, and on no occasion did he raise his voice or grow irritable. Having had no brothers and no father in a conventional sense, I had little idea how to bring up boys, but during the war I had been a strict mother. With Robin's return, I could see the two boys immediately copying him and therefore reinforcing what I had taught them. But there was a side of him, in common with many ex-soldiers at that time, which resented discipline: I can almost hear him saying now, 'Oh go to hell, I had enough of that in the war' – yet on the whole I think he had a grudging admiration for my wife-and-mother performance.

Just before Robin came back from Italy I had chosen Ashfold to be the boys' preparatory school, mostly because Jonathan Sieff was there, and Daphne and Michael thought highly of the school, particularly of James Harrison, its headmaster. From the start a boy was taught in the pattern he would have to follow when he went to public school. This gave him a sense of freedom and made him stand on his own feet at an early age. Jim Harrison also gave boys the chance to discover and love – if it was in them to do so – painting, music, literature and acting. I know our own sons, as they grew up, were grateful to him. Mr Creed (Old Creedo – he was actually quite young) taught painting and pottery, and Miss Ticehurst ('Tishy') taught the piano; this became Edward's lasting love.

Jim had a young and attractive girlfriend who mixed freely and happily with the children. I remember walking with them both on a windy, autumn day in the lovely park which surrounded the house and seeing – swaying in the wind on the top branch of a very tall tree – a boy spread-eagled; it seemed he might crash to his death any moment. I thought Jim hadn't seen him. Of course he had and turned to me, saying before I could speak: 'Keep quiet, walk on, take no notice whatsoever and all will be well.' We all three did exactly that and as I never heard of any accident, no doubt the child descended safely, oblivious to the fact his life had been in danger. This scene came back vividly much later during a conversation with David Niven, a friend more of Robin's than of mine. We had chartered a boat to go up the Thames for some theatrical party. David was very slightly on the wrong end of things at that time – he had grown older and there was a lull in his career, shortly to be overcome. He had been telling me about it and I had countered with 'Oh, but you're such a big star', when David said, 'That's the stickiest moment, you're happily spread-eagled on that top, swaying branch you've managed to claw and crawl to, and there you are, basking for a moment, having made the big-time in this damn-fool business, and some bloody fool opens his mouth and persuades you to do the wrong thing. In a second you're a gonner when it's taken you so long to get there.'

In the beginning I had found it hard to find the money for the fees at Ashfold. One day Elaine Blond called and discovered me crying myself into a jelly: the situation had got so bad that the local butcher wouldn't let me have any meat for the children. Elaine asked me how much money I needed. £300, I told her. 'I'll send it over,' she said but added that she was extremely angry I hadn't told her before. I, in my turn, became embarrassed and huffy and told her to take the money back, whereupon she asked me what the full scale of the problem was. Another time I confided to Daphne Sieff the straits I was in. She said, 'Tell Simon. I don't know what he'll do, but you'll get good advice.' She was right. Simon listened and immediately gave me half the sum I had named; he didn't lend it, he made it clear that he was giving it to me. As for the other half, he said he thought that with great care I could manage without it, and I would like myself better if I did. I did as he suggested, and learned a good and lasting lesson. I mention this to show the extent to which I had felt driven. Jim Harrison never worried or embarrassed me. He really loved his pupils and was not ashamed of the tear he brushed from his cheek when he listened to them singing Christmas carols.

John Turner was now a dear family friend. He came from the sort of family termed the 'back-bone of England'; his father was a comfortably off, respected man in the shipping business with a pleasant house at Ormskirk where we now stayed quite often in order to go to the Grand National. His mother was in failing health when we met her, and had to stay in bed a great deal, but when she heard I was interested in old china she leapt up like a schoolgirl and plunged into cupboards dotted about the house, crammed in a higgledy-piggledy way with a collection of Swansea, Bow, Minton, Rockingham . . .

John Turner inherited good looks from his parents. He was tall, ash blond, very pale, with blue eyes and a face as delicate and transparent as I had always imagined Rupert Brooke's to be. He was pedantic, almost precious, but he enjoyed Robin's company so much, was always very pleasant to me and took a great interest in our children. He was now head of the family business, married and settling for the life of a North Country businessman.

*

Simon, pleased that the career plan for his protégé was succeeding, now gave Robin and me a present – some money to use for a holiday. 'You should get away from your troubles and start afresh.' Robin's idea was that we should travel to Italy: he had left his heart there, that was why he delayed his return after the war, and he longed to go back just once . . . It was hardly starting afresh for us to bump all the way to Italy in John's vintage Bentley in order that Robin, with his wife in tow, should seek out an old love. I had a vision of him, in his perfect Italian, explaining:

I am here because I love you better than anyone else in the world, except my wife whom I have brought along, knowing she will understand, because she knows that I love her better than anyone else in the world.

How else was he going to explain my awkward presence, with John standing by as a sort of umpire?

We finally reached Andermatt where we were to cross the Swiss border into Italy. Simon Marks had told us before we left that Switzerland was still 'the oasis of Europe'. He was right. I was thrilled by the mountains and the snow, by the magically fresh air, and then quickly came down to earth and started to spend money in the shops; even packets of Kleenex were a joy. Only then did I realize the extent to which we had been short of everything for so long. To be able to buy as much butter as we wanted was a childish treat; I could not believe my eyes at such displays of food.

From Andermatt we set out for Stresa, where we were due to spend a day or two; Robin and John, when they finished their active service, had stayed for a while in Milan, so it was there we were headed. I would have liked to remain by the calm water of Lake Como for ever, but the two soldiers had to press on . . . In Milan they had lived in a flat belonging to an Italian woman in her early forties called Lara; Robin had talked about her a great deal, and showed me her photograph. She was lovely, tall, dark and pale-skinned, and sounded like a paragon. But I was very confused when I was told in Stresa, almost before we had unpacked, that Claudia, her daughter, would be arriving to join us. Arrive she did, young and fair, rather frail to look at, and deeply in love with my husband. John was told to look after me while Robin went to meet her. We did as instructed and took a boat on the lake, but on returning to the hotel, Robin and Claudia walked towards us, a most beautiful couple – I wondered why the hell I was there, and rather wished I was dead.

Anyway, we set out to meet Lara in Milan. She was delighted to see her old friends, and warm in her welcome to me. She was the daughter of an opera composer; we never discovered who was her husband. The flat was small but attractive if rather shabby. From the moment they walked in I had the feeling that Robin and John had arrived home, but I think it must have been clear to her that when Angela, the wife of her lover, was taken to meet her, the act was over. But had Robin been to bed with the daughter too? I was pretty well paralysed with misery and a sense of inadequacy during the rest of my first visit with Robin to Italy. He was perfectly civil and amiable to me; it might have been better if only I could have forgotten that I was supposed to be his wife. Had there only been one rival, perhaps I would have been expected to make a scene.

Robin took me on a tour, first to the Church of Santa Maria delle Grazie, to see 'The Last Supper' by Leonardo da Vinci, at that time badly damaged from the war. Viewing such a work in such conditions, still close in time as we were to the war, was an unforgettable experience. It made me feel how silly my worldly problems were.

Our next stop was the garage, not far from the cathedral, where Mussolini and his mistress had been executed. Robin gave me a graphic account of the killing. He showed me exactly where, after being shot, they had been strung upside down. He described Clara Petacci's courage when, after the whimpering Mussolini, it was her turn: refusing to be blindfolded, she leant nonchalantly against a wall, filing her nails until the firing squad took aim. Robin had been impressed by her and appalled by the deed: 'I wasn't important enough to stop them shooting her,' he said. But he would answer no questions. We toured the streets of Milan, and he showed me where fighting had taken place. He had appointments with mysterious, rich-seeming Milanese men who lived in spacious, dark apartments and must have been members of the same underground group. I couldn't say a word; the men were polite, but ignored me. They talked quietly and seriously with Robin. He never explained them and we never met them again.

The remainder of our holiday was spent outside Milan in a village called Orta, with a family who had befriended John and Robin called the Bettojas. The atmosphere there was peaceful. We ate too much pasta and fruit under the trees in their garden. We were waited on hand and foot by male and female servants who seemed to have been part of this family forever. We bathed in the lake, sometimes by moonlight. Had the war not touched them at all? Indeed it had. Sophia, the mother, was American; she had been in Rome, quite unable to leave when the Germans then occupied it. She was confined night and day to her apartment, where she hid her adolescent son, terrified that the Germans would take him and transport him to Germany. The only exercise the boy got was by walking short distances at dead of night near the flat: meantime Sophia would be rigid with fear that he would be caught. After our visit to Italy Robin's attitude that the war was over and must never be discussed again hardened. Perhaps he was right. Millions of people had suffered as we in England had never suffered: if they were fortunate enough to be alive, they never talked of it, but shrugged it aside.

Returning to England, it soon became clear that we were going in, not very well armed, to another type of fighting: the American entertainment industry was a struggle for money and power and human beings were pawns in that war, too.

7

Escape to New York

Zoë Gail sang, 'I'm going to get lit up when the lights go up in London', and in the same revue we suffered convulsions of laughter at the hands of a genius comedian called Sid Field. But it was the Americans who really took the curtain up for us again: Danny Kaye packed the Palladium to the roof for weeks on end in what was virtually a one-man show, and Howard Keel stormed on to the Drury Lane stage in *Oklahoma*, proclaiming 'Oh, what a beautiful morning'. Peace and a future were in the air.

The first of the big American stars Robin had dealings with were Jack Benny and Bob Hope. I was only permitted to meet them briefly, but we always had seats for their performances, and I shall never forget them. They were actors who made me feel justified again in being stagestruck, and my passion for the theatre, which had been extinct in wartime, was rekindled. Not surprisingly, with such names, MCA's one room in Dover Street began to bulge, and the Human Octopus was on the move. Its tentacles reached to Brook Street and encircled an already well-established agency called Linnet and Dunfee. Of the three partners, Bill Linnet, Jack Dunfee and Bill O'Brien, Bill Linnet was the one I knew best. He had worked in the theatre for many years, starting at the bottom, and had been general manager on tour with my old friend, Doris Rogers when I had been in *77 Park Lane*. When I met him he was the smoothest managing director in the West End, so I never told him this, thinking he would have no wish to be reminded of the past, particularly as one of his partners was an ex-Bentley boy, as the rich Brooklands racing drivers were called. Jack Dunfee was a very amusing man who knew as little about show business as is possible, though he was quite good at impressing pretty stagestruck girls; there was always one of these on his arm. He was a tall, balding, laconic, witty man who held most of the keys to the London jetset doors. I hardly knew Bill O'Brien. He had been in the Alexander Korda team, then married the actress Elizabeth Allen. He was a pleasant, haha man to me.

So eventually MCA absorbed all the Linnet and Dunfee clients and travelled on to acquire a fine house, 134 Piccadilly. Robin and Lol Evans were on the third floor; Linnet and Dunfee and their team were on the second floor; and the Octopus's prize morsel was on the first floor – Cecil Tennant, agent to the greatest stars of all, Vivien Leigh and Laurence Olivier. Tennant was a tall, good-looking man, very quiet in manner, who married the Russian dancer Irena Baronova. He was very close to Olivier in both his personal and professional life; in 1967, after Vivien Leigh's funeral, his car crashed into a tree and killed him – a tragic blow for Larry, but Lol Evans succeeded Cecil as his agent. Having already been manager at the New Theatre in 1945–6 he was ideal, and already represented other big stars such as Ralph Richardson and John Gielgud.

It was at this time that, ignoring what Robin had told me about not becoming involved in the business side of his life, I bluffed my way into buying antiques for Jules Stein, helping to furnish the MCA offices with valuable and beautiful furniture. 'Valuable' was the operative word with him: it applied both to human and inanimate objects. After all, you had to be smart to know when to acquire, or get rid of, either. By training I had as much right to be a buyer in the antique market as I had to dance a leading role in the Royal Ballet, but since childhood I had been surrounded by 'good pieces', as Harry and Glitters termed them, and had always loved them. Jules took me to lunch at Claridges; afterwards he tore me round the Antique Dealers' Fair. We arrived at the stands belonging to names like Mallet and Partridge of Bond Street, Blairman of Grafton Street, and he asked me what I liked. I said, 'Everything, of course,' not knowing how to be more specific. To my great relief, he barked, 'You're on.' So while he and Doris continued their globe-trotting, I bought antique furniture in England: pieces I paid infinitesimal amounts for are worth many thousands today.

With Jules Stein's money behind me, perhaps the wisest thing I did was to let dealers understand that I knew absolutely nothing and was not, in fact, qualified for my job. Everyone helped me a great deal and so I learned enough, later on, to open a shop in Beauchamp Place with Lord Middleton. I much preferred working for Americans: I liked their enthusiasm and sharpness of mind, and they were the best payers in the world. I cannot say the same for others, especially my own countrymen. This was an eye-opener of a most disturbing kind: rich people that one met socially exerted their fullest charm to avoid settling bills.

The reason I took a job was that Robin never opened a letter, never mind paying a bill: while he was marvellous at handling other people's financial affairs he couldn't be bothered with his own problems, and ignored them. His salary must have been fairly good but he spent a fortune on clothes. I must admit I loved the way he looked. He was now living just like his father Willie; the difference being that his income was not private but the Human Octopus's ten per cent; he was fast becoming the glamour boy of the showbiz world.

One example of his magnetic quality was his friendship with Robert Morley. Robert's love for 'Foxglove', as he nicknamed him, was instantaneous. Robin and I had gone backstage one matinée to see Leueen McGrath during a performance at the Lyric Theatre of *Edward, My Son*, written by Robert, in which Robert starred. I was sitting with Leueen and Robin had gone to see another actor a few dressing-rooms away. Robert Morley was making his way from his dressing-room to the stage to make an entrance and in the narrow corridor he and Robin actually collided. It is hardly an exaggeration to say that they were never apart again until Robin's coffin was lowered into the ground. Robert later wrote of Robin that he was a 'consummate actor: when dealing with the Italian film industry, a father of the Mafia; when arranging the affairs of the Royal Court Theatre for his great friend George Devine, a potentate of the Treasury; when gambling with me on the Riviera, a member of the Greek syndicate'. Robert also wrote that he was 'by far and away the most amusing friend I ever made'. When Robin could not afford the time to be with Robert, I became his stand-in and so the three of us formed a rich companionship with sometimes hilarious consequences.

Robin also had strong pulling power with English society women, a notoriously stagestruck breed. They could excuse their interest in him by saying, 'He's an old Harrovian, my dear, and a superb bridge player,' while their husbands closed one eye because 'He had a damned good war, and is a member of the MCC.' With those credentials no great harm could come, could it? And they could get on with their own lives, knowing their 'girls' were in safe hands. I grumbled bitterly when he turned his back on his own: I must have been a bore. At one time, I remember, I acted the typical injured wife because although his latest extra-marital love was very beautiful, she was stupid and tiresome beyond belief.

'Why her?' I wailed through my jealous tears.

'Because I am the good one in the relationship . . . she needs me.'

I heard what he meant and understood, but by then I was firmly set in the wife-and-mother mould.

Another affair failed to conform to the usual pattern and began to trouble me: the woman was the wife of a film director, a lively redhead, amusing, popular, hospitable – typically Irish – and well known for her enthusiastic affairs. She was ruthless but great fun; she loved her own children, almost smothering them with love. Robin was very much in love with her, and I saw every reason why this was so; I also knew that if she wanted to, she could destroy our marriage and take him away from the boys.

Preserving paternal stability for my boys was perhaps as important to me, if not more so, than keeping my husband, and I can truly state that in this regard I was very, very jealous of her, bitterly so – more than I can remember being over any other woman.

I consoled myself wryly that it was good to have faced such a tormenting emotion, and that my experience was yet again, thanks to Robin, being broadened.

*

Early in 1949 my American friend, Ronda Keane, Howard Jay Gould's daughter, invited me to spend the month of May with her in New York. I was thrilled and without hesitation accepted. Having discussed my forthcoming visit with Robin, I passed on to him the dollars Ronda sent to pay for my fare, knowing that a visa and a ticket could easily be arranged through his office. Alas for the straightforward view of things: Robin promptly spent the dollars on himself. I told Ronda and she sent the money a second time. This time *I* bought the ticket!

Looking back, I have the idea that Robin may have acted as he did because he didn't really want me to go. Perhaps he thought I might renew some, one in particular, of my wartime friendships. When I saw him, just prior to my departure, waving me goodbye outside the Pan Am building at Victoria, his expression was forlorn. Surely he couldn't really object to my departure for four weeks' much needed holiday? The gloomy farewell stirred guilt inside me. I checked my ticket and went through customs with an increasing sense of loneliness and apprehension; when, at last, the flight was called the joy felt in anticipation had vanished; I now thought perhaps I was wrong to go. Walking across the tarmac to the plane, I found myself shaking with extraordinary tension.

It seemed we were no sooner airborne than the captain announced we were landing in Ireland; we sat about in the gloomy airport lounge at Shannon gazing out on grey rain most of the day. In the afternoon we were called back to take our seats on board, and I got chatting to a fellow passenger, a building worker flying out to Bermuda. The captain's voice greeted us once more: this time, owing to some technical fault, we could not fly at the altitude he had promised. It was too late to turn back and he had to take the plane down low. I cannot say we had a bumpy flight, rather that we dipped and swayed just above a raging sea which appeared to reach up as if it would like to engulf us. My companion hated it every bit as much as I did but he was more sensible than I; he found some ugly grey blankets and put one over me, saying I ought to try and get some sleep. There was little chance of this: an elderly man a few seats ahead became desperately ill, so the pair of us occupied our time in observing the expertise, as well as kindness, lavished on him by the crew.

The night passed and another day of surprises was upon me. In those days your aeroplane broke the journey to New York at Gander in Newfoundland and here the early morning was cold and crisp, while the sun shone brilliantly in a blue sky. We were taken from the plane to a spotless restaurant where an obliging staff served fresh orange juice – the Dorchester served only tinned; real coffee – we subsisted on synthetic grains; porridge with real cream and a huge plate of bacon and eggs. This was followed by toast and marmalade until we could eat no more. What bliss!

Sustained by this wonderful breakfast in never-never land, it was with restored morale that we re-boarded our plane, certain in the knowledge that we would soon be in New York. Wrong again. Over the intercom again came the captain's voice: both the flight to New York and the landing there, he told us, were going to be very tricky. The city for miles around was shrouded in dense fog and something like three hundred aeroplanes were circling New York, taking their turn to land.

I was denied the exciting aerial view of New York but I was more than happy, hours later, to get through customs without the truculence and rudeness I had been told to expect. Very soon I found myself enjoying a warm welcome from Ronda and one of her father's lawyers, called Dan Woodhall. I had been travelling for ever, it seemed, yet every vestige of fatigue vanished: when my companions suggested that they motor me round town a little before we went to Ronda's apartment, I was thrilled. I cannot remember exactly where they took me but I know I fell in love with New York that day and that this love has never faded.

About mid-morning Dan dropped Ronda and myself at an apartment on East 54th Street, down near the river. She had rented this during my stay from an antique dealer friend, David Weiss, and it was perfection, right in the heart of New York. Ronda's black maid, Helen, was waiting with coffee. She unpacked my bags and ran me a bath and, when I thanked her, I heard for the first time the words I learned to treasure on this visit – 'You're welcome'. Hot baths are my favourite luxury, but the bath taken that morning on 54th Street comes top of the list of best bath memories. Ronda had to urge me to start to hurry a little as we were due to lunch with Howard at the Plaza, where he now lived permanently.

Being one of the richest men in America made Howard the nearest equivalent to being semi-Royal in England, so the hall porter bade us a most deferential welcome and told us that Mr Gould was waiting: we were taken through the room towards the great man with a tremendous flourish.

There was dear little Howard, all smiles and hugs and kisses; it was so good to be with him again.

Howard's new wife was also there. He had finally married a refugee actress, very much his junior, called Greta Mosheim, who had previously been married to Oscar Homolka. I remembered being at Mongewell Park when Greta, her mother, her sister and brother-in-law all arrived from Germany. Howard had taken charge of them and immediately fell in love with Greta, causing great consternation among his other lady loves. I had made Greta Edward's godmother, thinking that this would give her a feeling of belonging; I could have saved my energy – she remained unaware of the gesture.

The sun was shining and I could see Central Park, not at all the picture I had carried of New York in my imagination. I was surprised by the lack of ugly skyscrapers: the buildings on Fifth Avenue and Park Avenue and Madison Avenue were not overpowering, but examples of beautiful modern architecture. Also I was very struck by the light: day or night the light, natural or synthetic, seemed a kind of modern poetry.

A unique luxury that went with his family – highly unusual, even in America – was a chauffeur to drive us everywhere. However, Howard did conform to one American pattern, that of always having lawyers with him. Also at lunch was Henry Duckworth, Howard's solicitor in England, and Dan Woodhall. As a host, Howard got first prize. I shall never forget the size of the menu suddenly presented to me that morning. There was so much on it that we in England had forgotten, but I ordered what I usually ate at the Ritz: asparagus and hot lobster, followed by strawberries or raspberries and cream. Howard said he would like me to try the wine: he wasn't going to apologize because it was Californian, he would just like me to try. I had absolutely no difficulty there. As for the rest of that day, I do recall a sudden heat wave, when I knew that the village dressmaker had made me all the wrong clothes, but I hardly minded. I felt intensely happy, carefree in the midst of all this generosity. I presume that after lunch we made for the apartment on 54th Street, because I just remember going to bed.

*

Ronda had once been married to the son of Sir Patrick Hastings, the famous English KC. She had been very innocent but he had been something of a sadist. When she realized this the marriage broke up, and with the blessed facility rich people have to escape quickly, she left England and reverted to her American citizenship. She bought a house in Pennsylvania, and we set out there the following morning. The house was near a village called Doylestown, a good two hours' drive from New York, and the district was frequented by a great number of theatrical people, including Rodgers and Hammerstein. There was a good theatre at Bucks County in the district; a lot of plays and revues destined for New York were tried out there.

In the heart of the country, with a garden of about an acre and very reminiscent of England, Ronda's Doylestown house was white, half-timbered, and designed in Dutch Colonial style. On arrival I felt an almost overwhelming sense of serenity. In the Mongewell Park days she had been quite a stocky girl, a fine tennis player, quiet and amiable, but showing no satisfaction at being Howard's rather indulged, natural daughter. I am sure he adored her yet probably found it impossible to express his feeling, while on the other hand Ronda was overpowered by her glamorous mother, Doris Keane. A clever woman, of taste, Doris was a real loner, who, I think, found it far easier to be nice to me than even tolerant towards her own child. Since moving to America Ronda had lost all her stockiness, and I was now holidaying with a tiny, delicate, dark woman with very pale skin and immense, sad black eyes. She was a wonderful companion and her generosity to me was entirely selfless.

At this point my former boyfriend telephoned me and we spoke for some minutes, but as I had been too often the wife of a husband looking over his shoulder at a past love, I lost all desire to play that game myself. We talked pleasantly enough; I am sure he was as relieved as I was that we did not meet again.

Neville and Elaine Blond were also in New York, living at the Drake Hotel. They were eminent and cosmopolitan. Neville had an important Board of Trade job, generating success for England and himself, but Elaine found living at even a good hotel very trying: 'slumming' was her word for it. 'In what way?' I asked. 'Well, for instance, I have to wash my own stockings.' I never found a suitable answer to that.

Neville, with his usual largesse, was heard to say, 'We'll go anywhere you fancy, Angie: all doors are open to me.'

'21,' I answered in a flash: I'd heard so much of this famous restaurant and had met the Burns brothers who owned it when they and their wives had visited England. Very quickly on this trip I had become a thorough glutton, rising each morning and saying to myself, 'I'm going to eat steak, not black-market horse.' So off we went with the Blonds to dinner: the food was absurdly rich, the rest of the clientèle absurdly spoiled, with the men noisy and drinking far too much, the women all looking as though they'd stepped straight off the cover of *Vogue*. I assume the British Government paid for this outrageously expensive outing; Neville kept telling me how short of money they kept him, not that I saw much sign of it.

The next high spot of my visit was seeing Leueen McGrath again, who had gone to New York in *Edward, My Son* and remained there after it closed. Her part, that of the secretary with whom the tycoon has an affair, had not been large but it was showy and even in the street she was recognized and greeted. Now she lived in New York as if she was a big star and, moreover, she was just about to marry George Kaufman, the famous playwright. Leueen, a dotty, generous Irish girl, had elegant looks and an ability to indulge in rather highfalutin, intellectual talk, both of which were irresistible to New Yorkers.

As soon as she told me she was going to marry George Kaufman, I asked her if he had given her any money.

'Not a penny.'

'You're mad. Americans expect to give their women money – before anything else.'

'You're a disgusting materialist. Get out. I never want to see you again.'

Laughing, I left Leueen. We understood each other perfectly; she knew how it was all very well for me to talk – I was less likely even than her to be clever on that score. I strolled back to 54th Street, a few blocks away. Only a short while later the front bell rang: enter a bubbling, radiant Leueen clutching a great thick roll of dollar bills. She flung some towards me. 'Oh, Angela, George came in just after you left . . . there you are, darling, half for me, half for you!' So we made some tea and planned how we would fritter away all this lovely money on dresses at Bergdorf Goodman or wherever. And we made plans for her marriage, which was due to take place at George's country home, near Ronda's.

George's apartment in New York was magnificent and gloomy, though soon Leueen was to alter all that. Perhaps he was a kind and good man – all the famous Broadway names certainly turned up for the marriage – but I found him dark, ugly, and saturnine, altogether unlovable. His plays were very good, very witty, but I never in any circumstances heard him make a funny remark. I suppose all he longed to be, all he had to say, he put into his plays: he wanted you to know him that way and no other. I was baffled as to how my friend could even contemplate marrying him: I laughed with her about his money and power but he was always kind to her.

The marriage ceremony was black farce. It took place in the drawing-room of his country house and there were so many flowers it looked like a funeral parlour. I kept thinking, there must be a body under all those flowers. Moss Hart the playwright, his wife Kitty Carlisle, Michael Kidd, the choreographer, were there, and many famous names. The person I most recall was the writer Edna Ferber. Ugly, strong and aggressive, she was such a contrast to Leueen, who had rather gone to town on bridal vestments. The illustrious guests stood around very conscious of their fame and sophistication: show business aristocracy was born just as the other type, on our side of the Atlantic, was dying out. Ronda and I loved it all. I kept whispering in her ear 'Who's that, who's that?' George showed not a glimmer of humour on his wedding day, though his daughter Anne was friendly. I'd better add that George never did me an ounce of harm: at the end of his life I even felt my heart touched by his unhappiness. I saw him once again in a Little Venice house in London which had been made exquisite by Oliver Messel. He struck me as being so alone, so unable to communicate, that just to look at him saddened me.

Ronda and I returned soon after this wedding to New York. We had a week of theatre-viewing: Alfred Drake in *Kiss Me Kate*; Lee J. Cobb in *Death of a Salesman*; Henry Fonda in *Mr Roberts*.

The best performance of all was Rex Harrison as Henry VIII in *Anne of a Thousand Days*. I saw this at a matinée during a heat-wave: the weight of the costumes alone would have daunted most actors, but Rex was poetic, sensitive, and strong. A ruthless and evil character, Henry, sure, but when he prayed downstage as Anne, touchingly played by Joyce Redman, was beheaded, Rex was as moving as anything I'd ever witnessed. Afterwards I found him delighted to see me once more. I'd known him for many years, since I was seventeen and shared theatrical digs with him in Glasgow. At that time he was playing the lead in another play – he wore suede shoes and a monocle – and he was in love with a girl in my company. I thought he liked me until one day I returned to the digs alone. A window was open, the breeze had blown a piece of paper to the floor; addressed to his girl-friend it read: 'Christine, get rid of this little Worthington girl or I shall leave you – she's driving me mad!' Not, you might think, a good prelude to a friendship that has lasted over fifty years.

Rex was now going through one of his patches of woman trouble – some gorgeous girl in Hollywood had slit her wrists and taken an overdose to the accompaniment of much publicity. Apparently she had been desperately in love with Rex. The whole scandal was causing him great distress, and my own warmth towards him and neutrality amid the general press hostility I hope comforted him. I always think of Rex as a great actor far more sinned against – or talked sinfully about – than sinful.

The climax to our invigorating playgoing was *South Pacific* with Mary Martin and Ezio Pinza; this was so enjoyable that I returned with Ronda to 54th Street totally oblivious of any of life's problems, real or imagined. I found a note on the telephone pad in Helen's handwriting to say that Mr Fox and Mr Morley were arriving at La Guardia at 11.00 the following morning, and would I please be there to meet them.

8

And Back Again

It never entered my head for a moment to leave a message at the airport to say where the two of them could find me on their arrival, and then to continue, at least until they turned up, with my new self. Foolish of me, because in those early days of flying aeroplanes were no more likely than today to arrive on time. So I hung about La Guardia all day and when at last the weary travellers emerged I was as jaded and cross as they were, particularly Robin.

Robert Morley lives with a quip or a joke on his lips, so he immediately said, 'A lovely trip, dovikins, such a nice aeroplane, it had a spiral staircase leading straight into the sea.' He is a man, anyway, who has spent his entire life seeking reasons to board aeroplanes, often with no other aim than to find a different casino to indulge his mania to gamble away his wonderfully hard-earned money. 'Shall we go to Nice, darling, or Moscow, or Corsica, or Sydney?' – or wherever else he feels drawn by his restless temperament. He has gone almost before the idea is voiced, if necessary alone but for preference dragging the willing or, better than nothing, the unwilling, with him.

But there are two sides to this huge restlessness of a huge man. Robert loves playing 'Happy Families', too, with much love and energy poured into endlessly praising and dominating his own family. He is married to Joan, Gladys Cooper's eldest child, whom I had known at Birchington. She is a marvellous homemaker. At their house in the country there is always a table groaning with food at which Robert can sit at the head and play big, funny Daddy; but then, at a moment's notice, and very often, he will announce to any likely candidate for escape: 'We're off!' Joan appears to remain totally unmoved by Robert's capers; her unquestioning acceptance of his peregrinations has always fascinated me: the sun rises and sets on her family.

Robert's urge to travel this time had been inspired by me: he prefers all pairs to observe the rules of being happily married, and he had the idea that I had come to New York to see some man. 'Oh dear,' he must have thought to himself, 'perhaps Foxglove's marriage is looking a bit wonky' – and himself felt like a change, anyway. Had I been seeing another man, he would soon have put a spanner in the works. By this time our friendship had expanded considerably, and Robert would address me variously as 'Mrs Walter Mitty Fox', 'Mother Superior', or 'Angela Onassis'. As it was, his and Robin's arrival in New York ruined my holiday but Robert's first priority was to protect Robin.

I was later somewhat hurt – something I hate to admit – when Robert gained some amusement, at least, from Robin's philanderings and never, with regard to these, showed me the faintest loyalty. At one time he used to be particularly helpful to the husbands of girls he had an eye to, always pleading for understanding and tolerance to be shown to them and often taking them on his jaunts: 'Such a nice fellow, darling, she really shouldn't criticize him.' I have longed for just one husband to stand up to him, but they never do.

For the present all three sides of our triangle were strained. Robin and Robert had a double room at the Algonquin and planned to be in New York for about three days. Robert offered to pay the difference in my fare to have me return with them, since by this time they had realized their journey was unnecessary, but I still had over a week's holiday left and made it clear to both of them that I wasn't going to cut things short. I wanted to show them my new clothes, as I was well-dressed for the first time in years, but that didn't go down well either.

Still, they made the best of it. Robert disappeared and Robin did some work at MCA with Kay Brown; when he and I met in the evening he was contrary and irritable for the most part, telling me how much he loathed New York (he loved it just as much as I did) and how all the plays I enthused about were second-rate rubbish. Once he and Robert had been reassured that I really wasn't going to run away, there seemed little else to talk about.

They left again, as arranged, for London, after I had given them the number of the flight I would be on in due course, but Robin had succeeded in taking the gilt off my own, very unsophisticated gingerbread. I told Ronda, who understood perfectly, that I would like to spend the remaining time in Doylestown; this was a fortunate decision because I then had the good fortune to spend a day with Ronda's architect, 'Wales' Bowman, and his friend the distinguished theatre critic, Stark Young, with whom I found I had an immediate rapport.

Rex Harrison had closed in *Anne of a Thousand Days*, and he and I had arranged that we would fly back to London on the same plane. Rex and Lilli Palmer, his first wife, were now divorced but she had also decided that she would fly to London with him; the fourth in our party was the actor Jack Merivale, Gladys Cooper's stepson from her third marriage, who later became Vivien Leigh's devoted friend and comforter. By now the weather had warmed up and the heat on the day of departure was intense. During that last morning Ronda was looking very frail. I was standing with her on Lexington when suddenly she had a tremendous attack of coughing and I saw the handkerchief she put to her mouth was covered in blood. It was only then she told me she had tuberculosis and that she was being admitted to hospital that same afternoon. I was furious with myself for being such a selfish, unobservant idiot; what had I ever done to deserve such a dedicated friend?

I was relieved to hear later that Ronda's story had a happy ending. She entered a chest clinic where, after many weeks, her health was restored. She was in the care of a Carl Muschenheim; he looked after her so well that she grew to like and depend on him and was very distressed when he told her he thought she ought to convalesce at a clinic in Arizona. She argued and remonstrated, but he was adamant. She wrote me that although she knew she was physically better, she found no joy at this as she missed Muschenheim's encouragement and understanding more than she had thought possible. I felt for her, so it was good to receive a further letter: Carl had suddenly walked into her room in the Arizona Clinic, had stood at the foot of her bed and said, 'I sent you away because I'd fallen in love with you, and one must never fall in love with a patient. My marriage was unhappy and had been for years. That had nothing to do with you, but now my divorce has gone through. I am free, will you marry me?' She did.

*

It seemed that easy transatlantic journeys were not meant for me: this time we had to make a forced landing at Goose Bay, where we were not even told how long we might be delayed. In arctic conditions we sat on packing cases, having dragged out whatever bits and pieces we could find from our hand luggage in a wholly unsatisfactory effort to keep warm. We played gin rummy, and as I am the worst of all card players the trip got expensive as well as bitterly cold. I had great reason to admire Rex; with more problems than most of us, he was by far the most humorous and disciplined of all.

Robin was at the airport to meet me. He was a sad, ill-looking, almost shabby edition of himself. The journey from the airport passed in absolute silence, and I was able to see with clarity how insensitive and self-obsessed I had become. I didn't regret running away to America – for running away it was, though I could call it what I liked – the need for a change, a rest, the necessity to sort things out. Of course the war years had been difficult, though less so for me than for millions of others: I had enjoyed being the fairy on a rather unstable Christmas tree for a long time, and had found coming down to earth difficult.

Self-pity over this and other factors had obscured my awareness of Robin's need for things that sound old-fashioned: domesticity, understanding, affection, time to heal the mental traumas we had all been through, time, in particular, to recover his health and heal the horrendous wounds he had sustained and never mentioned. These were the things he had really needed but never asked for.

I know now that to my immediate reaction on seeing the apparently wholly exhausted man who came to meet me – 'Oh God, where do we go from here?' – there was no immediate answer; but at the same time, to my surprise, I felt love for him such as I had never felt before, and this never left me.

So we were able to talk briefly for the first time as grown-up people: we discussed the lives we thought we wanted for ourselves and for our children. Despite the fact that I had not been very helpful to him, Robin was doing extremely well at MCA. I was able to take stock not only of his situation, but also of my own, and I came to the conclusion, without conceit, I hope, that he liked me very much, that he always had. After all, I was the one he had married, and he could have got out of it.

I accepted, although not too happily, that there would always be some romance on the side: he had an essential need for this, and for me to react in a certain way. As the years went by, I often used to re-encounter his conquests and even became friends with some of them; but, given a lapse of time, Robin would forget them completely. He would ask me the name of the girl I was talking to, and when I reminded him, remonstrating and calling him an insensitive, cruel man, he would laugh at me and later tell the story against himself with amusement. His sister, Pamela, was probably right when she said to me during one rather difficult period, 'Oh, he'll never leave you. You need have no worry. It's his Jewish side. Wives are always safe.'

Anyway, to finish my stock-taking in June of 1949, I knew that Robin and his work, his hobbies and his interests must from now onwards come first. That was not unselfish, it was the way I wanted it, the life that would make me happy – not, perhaps, a truth about any woman that I would have much success in teaching a girl today. But soon my plans began to work. We enjoyed the same plays and were moved by the same music. He was a good games player; I was hopeless but actually enjoyed watching him and his friends even play bridge. I enjoyed the dinner parties that I either gave or attended preceding these games, and the drives home were fun because I had been watching and listening to people all evening. As we drove, I would listen to Robin summing up, and find myself delighted at the points I had missed: for me that made him very companionable. Robin never judged people, he just saw them as they were. I think he was rather nicer than me: I was always turning my geese into swans, and he very often loved his geese best.

*

The most important thing of all was that we shared our children.

One day Robin was seeing Irene Howard – the actor Leslie Howard's sister who was MGM's casting director in England. Robin had been wanting to talk about a client but Irene said to him, 'Don't bother me with that, find me an attractive ten-year-old boy to be the son of Greer Garson and Walter Pidgeon in *The Miniver Story*.'

Impatiently Robin answered, 'Oh, have one of mine. Look, here are their photographs.'

'Snap,' said Irene. 'Bring them to the studio tomorrow.'

It was the school holidays and so we told the boys about this quite light-heartedly, thinking nothing would come of it. Off we went to Metro-Goldwyn land.

The producer, Sidney Franklyn, and the director immediately thought both boys were 'just perfect' so suddenly it was a question, almost laughingly, of which was to be the lucky lad. This didn't take long either, because Edward fled from the office, saying something like, 'I'm not going to do anything disgusting like that.' But James said, 'I'd love a go, I think it would be great fun.' And so there he was, engaged on the spot.

The moment Walter Pidgeon saw him he said, 'Well, there's going to be nothing I can do to get noticed in this picture.'

Shooting was supposed to take about six weeks; it finally took six months and James was paid a great deal of money – comparatively, that is. It was certainly nothing to do with James that shooting the film took so long: whatever scenes he had to play were always shot with the minimum number of takes. From the day we arrived he was completely at home with the camera, a gift he has retained.

James and I were established at the Berkeley Hotel with a Rolls Royce calling for us every morning at dawn to take us to the MGM studios in Elstree. In the beginning it was all rather a novelty. It interfered with his schooling but a young master from Ashfold was delegated to be his tutor and when not working James was supposed to have lessons, but this was very difficult to fit in. Although he had a nice dressing-room where it was possible for him to be quiet, no small boy could be cooped up in a soulless, impersonal room for any length of time, and the very able technicians connected with the film were terribly patient and kind to him.

Greer Garson was always totally professional. I had first seen her when she was a rather gorgeous, flamboyant redhead, being intently civil one weekend at the Simon Marks's country house to a very nice man, Cecil Madden, who was one of the heads of the BBC. I never saw her again until she was a great star, cool, quiet, disciplined and enigmatic. As Mrs Miniver she looked lovely and behaved impeccably, but I don't believe she spoke one friendly word to us for the whole of the six months. Walter Pidgeon, on the other hand, was equally professional but a most relaxed and friendly man. The script had been written by Ronald Millar – now Sir Ronald – who was most warm and kind, as indeed was pretty well everyone connected with the picture. It was a Hollywood extravaganza and the studios in those days were vast: one of them, where James was working, represented most impressively an entire English village shrouded in snow.

James's chief reaction to becoming a boy film star was boredom. His greatest ambition, like any other boy, was to have a new bike, and so for him the best day in those long and tedious six months was when we went into Elstree one lunchtime and bought the one he wanted. Before he had even finished *The Miniver Story* for MGM, James was already contracted through us to make another film, *The Magnet*, for Ealing Studios. Some days when shooting had been mainly centred on him and his tiredness became really sad, he would say, 'Everything is crowding in on me, it's all on top of me. Please get them away from me.' He was under contract, however, he was committed and, having been around the business all my life, I knew there was no way to escape the schedule.

Luckily, I could talk to and explain the problem to the director and later, in the case of *The Magnet*, to the producer, Sidney Cole, and could alleviate the pressures on him slightly. But it was never enough.

Part of *The Magnet* was quite different and much happier: when James was working in Liverpool on location, he and I lived with the rest of the unit at the Victoria Hotel in Wallasey. We breakfasted at big tables in the hotel before the other guests had even been called with their morning tea, and every morning and evening we went back and forth to Liverpool on the ferry. James was joined in his work by a group of local, working-class schoolchildren: they all got on well together and Charles Frend, the director, encouraged this, turning the scenes into a great adventure for them and capturing this in his picture, one of the reasons why, although a small film, it was a success.

Where Liverpool Cathedral now stands was a derelict bomb site and while the next scene was being set up – a long and exhausting process for grown-ups, worse still for children – endless cricket matches were played with anyone who could spare a moment to join in. Sidney Cole used to tell me he was a communist, but I didn't disapprove because he loved cricket. One of the first things he told me was that he could get us seats at the Oval for the next Test Match. I also liked Kay Walsh, who was James's film mother.

Back at Ealing, there was still some shooting to be done. Here I first noticed Michael Balcon, pillar of the British film industry – then an industry which created work for many and a happy escape for millions. He never came near the set, never talked to us. I recollect a man sitting at a table in the canteen we all used, eating a lonely meal – rather a stocky, balding man, with a moustache. I never heard him utter a word or saw anyone go up to speak to him. Like George Devine he seemed to be a magnet to young and talented people, recognizing their potential and helping it to flower. Neither man sought personal praise – they were happy to remain father figures: once their protégés were on their feet they would leave them to get on with it and gather praise as if they had done it alone.

While we were finishing *The Magnet* at Ealing, I vowed never again – no more filming, ever, for James. This remained the situation for twelve years until the child grew into a young man, changed his name and made *The Servant.*

I was helped greatly in the decision I made about his return into being an ordinary schoolboy by Charles Frend, director of *The Magnet.* He told me that James was really talented and could do anything that was asked of him, could convey through the camera every thought and subtle mood with the minimum of effort both to himself and to the technicians involved. He insisted that these gifts would not wane and that it was a foolish life for a little boy. I heeded his advice.

Of course being the mother of a child star had an appeal: I now see that the person who got most out of James's stardom was myself. Living at the Berkeley or, later, at the Savoy, I was cocooned from all the problems of home and marriage. I did not see clearly, as I do now, how much James missed and needed his friends: he did not tell me and had, I think, no way of doing so. His father and I must have been very obtuse.

We returned at last to reality. James went back to Ashfold and I to Cuckfield, where Alice had managed perfectly well without me. James's name was often in the papers – 'He Had Worked on a Film' but he must not mention it at school, that would be swanking and there were boys, anyway, who were jealous and who, however modest he was, took it out on him. Even some masters resented his coming and going. I fought some battles on his behalf, unwisely I think: the situation would have resolved itself and, by interfering, I helped worsen it.

Edward, too, must have found all this a bit difficult. He must have envied James at least a shade at first and he may then have felt sorry for this lucky brother, having to come back to the difficulties James had to face. At the time I had absolutely no thoughts along these lines: it is only now that I know how stupid parents are, how little they know, or choose to know, about their children's problems.

PART THREE

9

A Sense of Direction

Edward and James were joined by Robert, born on 25 March 1953. Cocky Farr, our local doctor, had a great reputation in this field and I knew it was justified. I thoroughly enjoyed the birth – in fact it was accompanied by laughter. Robert was born in about four hours. Robin had been told what was happening, and walked in within minutes of the baby being born. He seized him as soon as he could and waltzed round the room, humming the Blue Danube. He suddenly stopped, looked at him and said, 'My God, he's exactly like Sid Mitchell.' I don't think he looked like 'my Sid' – which was what Alice always called her husband.

As Robin became more popular at MCA he was persuaded by pressure from clients to give up the legal side entirely and become purely an agent; in his case more a personal manager. The playboy side of him, now he had got it under control, was something he could actually use and he became a workaholic, immensely caring, personally involved with and dedicated to his artists and their needs. He confessed that the more difficult his clients were, the more he enjoyed them; he often told me: 'I love them you see.' He did, and sometimes they loved him.

He had now got over the rather childish idea that I must never meet the people he worked for. Robin was John Osborne's agent and also Paul Scofield's. Paul lived in the next village to us and I saw him continually. Paul never stayed a night in London.

We would often travel to London together and whenever we encountered each other on the platform at Haywards Heath would launch into theatre talk. One day he was going up to play King Lear and we boarded the train, talking hard. We paused after a while, realizing that the train had come to a halt. I remember Paul looking sharply at his watch. He must be punctual – the make-up for King Lear took a lot of time and effort. The train was strangely quiet and absolutely stuck. Sensing his controlled anxiety, I opened the window and looked out. Our journey had come to a dead end: the train was facing a huge, solid, brick wall. Talking too much, we had boarded the wrong train and were stranded at a tiny station called Horsted Keynes. Now Paul surprised me. He accepted without demur that he would not reach the theatre on time, that the understudy would go on, so he simply went on talking.

James (Jimmy) Woolf, brother of Sir John Woolf, was another client; the Woolfs were the head of Romulus Films and made some of the better known pictures to come out of British studios. Jimmy was making *Room at the Top* when I first met him, and I used to visit the set with him quite often; he was a tireless professional. He liked to go to the studio when *Room* was being shot as his beloved friend, Lawrence Harvey, was playing the lead; he always referred to Harvey as 'Centre Piece'.

Jimmy came from a rich Jewish family. He was a highly educated, clever man but was a loner and lived in a suite at Grosvenor House. He had a grave problem which all who knew him and were fond of him tried to overlook: he was heavily on drugs. I always knew this and, for the only time in my life that I can remember, I made a real effort to pretend that perhaps I was wrong in disapproving. We would dine with him often or, if Robin was away, I would go out with him on my own to the Caprice. I used to join him at Grosvenor House first, where lots of his friends used to drop in. He was particularly fond of Terence Stamp, always known as 'T', who was, at that time, linked romantically, by the newspapers anyway, with the top model Jean Shrimpton. Wicked Jimmy was not nearly as nice to her as he was to 'T'; still, he had such humour and he was such good company that there was nothing I wouldn't forgive him.

We also used to see John and Mary Mills quite often; they were clients of Lol Evans's, but we stayed with them and they with us because our children were friendly. I think of Mary as a great home-maker, a bigger role than actress and writer – which she also was – and of both of them as generous hosts. The whole family was fun to be with and, when the children were young, we had happy holidays with them at a house at Sandwich.

Our most interesting older client was the Hungarian George Tabori. He had been a close friend of Bertolt Brecht and Kurt Weill, and had got together a very good programme at the Royal Court about their work. He lived at Cuckfield with us for months at a time, Robin being convinced he was a great writer. He was indeed a brilliant writer – with a Hungarian genius for unreliability, though this never troubled Robin at all who thought his book, *Portrait of the Left Hand*, one of the best novels written about the war. George, for us, did everything wrong, but it didn't matter: he was an eccentric who inspired great affection. He also wrote a play which failed but which had the first big part that Peter Sellers played – Sellers was totally unsuitable for the role but George's play made people realize he was a genius. George wrote many things when he stayed at Cuckfield, including *Secret Ceremony*, directed by Joe Losey, a vehicle for Elizabeth Taylor: the most important scene was based on the fact that my mani-curist went off her head instead of manicuring my nails.

Paul Scofield often came by and our only periods of peace from George's incessant tapping of the typewriter was when Paul arrived to take him for a walk. I can hear my maid, Mary, calling 'Mr Tabs, Mr Tabs (her name for George), come off your ticcatiboo, Mr Sco has come to take you for a walk.' It's difficult to describe George; he was lazy, gentle, hypochondriacal, observ-ant, wise and loving. Of course, he had suffered in ways that I could never understand. His father was killed in front of him in Budapest: his mother had been in Dachau; his brother, Paul, was a refugee in London but established himself as a successful writer. George later moved to Berlin, and is now the guru of West Berlin theatre; Edward, filming there recently in *Wild Geese II*, in place of Richard Burton, saw much of him.

*

It was in the early 1950s that Robin, through our friend Neville Blond, became involved in the Royal Court Theatre. George Devine and his work for this theatre became the strongest interest, even the passion, of my husband's life. Neville Blond had become the Chairman of the Royal Court. He had no knowledge of, and no great love for, the theatre, but Chairman was a function he understood: he knew where the money was, the mischievous fellow, and he was going to get it. He succeeded, even while a lot of people he got it from disapproved of the venture. Neville recognized that George had an immensely important contribution to make but had no idea what made him tick, so he needed a middleman to bridge the gulf between them, and he chose Robin. These three very different men, as well as feeling mutual respect, also found room to form a real friendship and a unique team which, with all the talent George Devine gathered round him and inspired, altered the face of the English theatre and opened the door for a host of brilliant unknowns to make their entrances.

No book I have read about George Devine or the Royal Court reports accurately what happened: some of the writers do not even know the names of those involved or show the slightest inclination to learn them. For example, Alan Tagg designed twenty-seven plays, including *Look Back in Anger*, and he has never been asked one single question. He knows possibly more about the people involved, the successes, the failures and the difficulties of the enterprise than anyone else in the business. From Alan I have learned not only of the inspiration provided by George, whose philosophy for his Company was 'You have a right to fail', but also, equally important, of the hard work done backstage by those who designed, made and painted the scenery, set the wigs, fixed the lighting and stitched the costumes. At the Court, these people worked in the greatest discomfort in sheds at the back.

The more glittering and well-publicized parts of the operation were the fund-raising cocktail parties and other meetings generously hosted by the Marks & Spencer family at the firm's headquarters in Baker Street. The drink flowed and the canapés were delicious. Many members of the family were prominent on a raised platform, dishing out speeches to encourage this worthwhile artistic endeavour. But I never saw any sign of the big cheques, widely thought to be crucial to the life and survival of the Royal Court, resulting from these parties. Committee meetings were conscientiously attended and much was courageously criticized, often provoking disapproval among those actually working in the theatre.

Neville had persuaded Robin to join him because he needed Robin's legal background. Robin loved both George Devine and Neville and sensed he could be of genuine use as a liaison officer; his frustrated childhood longing to be an actor, which had never left him, found an outlet working in Sloane Square. This period of his life was his happiest, and his reward was the loyalty and devotion of everyone concerned with the birth and brief flowering of the Royal Court.

He began with an annual salary of £1000, a sum worth having at that time, but soon after he had disagreed with some decision of Neville's or perhaps with his attitude to George, he tore up his contract in pieces as small as confetti, scattering them all over Neville.

Horrified, Neville told him: 'You can't do that, you can't leave us.'

'I'm not leaving you,' replied Robin. 'I'm staying to support George in what I think this is all about, but I'm not staying to act as your yes-man.'

It says much for Neville that he was absolutely delighted by this attitude: it was exactly the sort of thing he would have done himself, had he been in the same situation, and the affection these two men felt for each other became stronger than ever.

Neville was a dark, swarthy, even ugly man, with wide cheek-bones and eyes which were watchful and amused. He used to get all the information he wanted by pretending to know nothing and asking questions. He had great charm, so this would flatter the subjects of his enquiry, who would then fill him in on all he needed to know – and often a great deal more besides. He could judge which information was the truth – and therefore useful, and much that he learned he kept to himself. He had a large experience of the rough as well as the smooth of life, and recognized instantly signs of difficulty or stress in a person, no matter how efficient the camouflage. If he thought material assistance would help, he saw that help was forthcoming. This was always anonymous, which might be considered odd because he was a flamboyant personality. He was a good host, and fun to be with.

I could never have guessed George Devine was an actor, and a very good one at that, when I first met him. Physically he looked like a farmer. He already had white hair and very sharp, watchful brown eyes. I remember going back one day to our flat to find he was having drinks. I had been at a long and distressing meeting at the National Adoption Society, where I had worked voluntarily for many years. He noticed at once that I was feeling or looking flat. 'And what ails you?' he asked. I told him of the plight of a child I had long been interested in, who had, that day, been taken from its adoptive parents with whom it had been flourishing, and given back on a Court Order to its natural mother. She, I felt, did not want it and would never love it because she was a hard woman. 'Oh,' said George, 'I never knew you were interested in doing anything useful.' I do hope he wasn't right, even though he was a very shrewd man!

Though I'd given up my antique shop to have Robert, I kept myself well away from the Royal Court Theatre; but at home Robin would discuss every angle of it with me for hours at a time. I was never as enthusiastic about the productions as he was, for I was old-fashioned and liked to see stars. I never said so, of course, yet George could well have sensed it: he wasn't one to miss a trick.

At our London flat not only George but many others who worked at the Court would turn up frequently. Many of the Royal Court troupe also came to Ockenden, either to stay or to join the lunch parties we gave most Sundays. Some came to get restored if they weren't very well. Nicol Williamson was a friend of Edward's; they had been at Dundee Repertory Theatre together. Nicol was a great hypochondriac and Edward had told him that Cocky Farr was the doctor he needed. Nicol said he had jaundice, so an appointment was made. Cocky examined him and the diagnosis was: 'Nothing wrong with Nicol Williamson but Nicol Williamson.' He was restored at once. Before he'd gone to Cocky, he'd been looking at himself steadily in the mirror in my sitting room, and putting out his tongue gloomily. Now it was all change: the mirror reflected a handsome, vibrant actor, glowing with health. He kept combing his rather sparse, reddish-blond hair and threatened to sing me some popular songs: he was better than Elvis Presley, he said, and about to prove it with a one-man show.

The following week a good client of Robin's arrived saying he, too, had jaundice; he also was accompanied by Edward and had received the same talk on the infallible Farr. This patient was Anthony Page, the director. As we were then, and I still am, very fond of him, I think he will forgive me when I admit that on telephoning Cocky to make the appointment I said, 'I have another hypochondriac with jaundice for you to see. His name is Anthony Page. He is rather special, so nice and clever.' Cocky saw him, made the examination and came back with: 'I agree Anthony Page is nice, clever, and very special; he also has such bad jaundice that his liver may be impaired.'

Another invalid was Peter Gill. He stayed for quite a time and really had been seriously ill. Possibly the cleverest of George Devine's troupe, he had been a particular protégé of Sophie Devine's and his production of the D. H. Lawrence plays was remarkably good. Peter was delicate, so I'm pleased to see that his position at the National Theatre must mean that he's overcome his health problems. William Gaskill, another client, brought Peter to the house on the first visit. I laughed because Robin and Bill could have had nothing in common – Robin described him as an intellectual, the only true one in the theatre. Intellectual Robin was not, but they got on very well, and I expect Bill enjoyed having a down-to-earth business manager. Often, I admit, I didn't know what the hell Bill was talking about. He was a sloppily dressed, watching man; difficult to communicate with, full of strong prejudices – a lot of them to do with something called 'class' which I always find irritating. But I am full of affection for him: when I was first on my own, he invited me out for lunch to a very expensive restaurant. It was not his scene at all and we had very little to say to each other, but of all the group he was the one who issued this kind invitation.

Tony Richardson came under Robin's wing, and so we were invited to his domaine, Nid du Duc, in the south of France. The Cannes Film Festival was in progress and we were due to meet Tony, who was coming to Nice from the East, at the Terrace Bar of the Carlton Hotel; Robin thought it a good opportunity to see several clients at the same time. It was dreadfully hot. One of Tony's hobbies was collecting rare birds, and he had bought some on his Eastern trip. Rather cleverly, he had now parked his car near the bar, so we had a good view of it. There were birds locked up on top of one another, with no air getting to them, and they had been given no water, while the sun was beating mercilessly down. Tony was in good form, his rather hysterical laugh well to the fore. He was a highly strung young man who had been assistant to George Devine at Stratford-on-Avon, and had gone to the Royal Court with him; for me he was *un enfant*-a-little-too-*terrible*. I felt agitated at the plight of his birds, and when he appeared not even to hear my pleas for shade, air, and water for them, my agitation turned to anger and dislike for the man who was going to be my host for a week. A bad start to a holiday.

The house Tony lived in, the biggest in the domaine, was

quite ordinary – remarkably like a seaside house rented for school holidays – but dotted around the estate of farmland and olive groves were dug-out caves in the rocks, originally for housing shepherds, which had been converted into studios. Tony said David Hockney was in one and Mick Jagger in another. We never saw hide nor hair of them, but that was Tony's story. Mick Jagger had once been to see Robin at Cuckfield when he was in some trouble or another in the early days. He had seemed quiet and well-mannered but I remember, while the two of them were talking at dinner, gazing on this raw-featured, pasty youth and wondering why the young of the world loved him.

Ni le Duc was a mixture of unspoiled beauty, with a natural waterfall and river running through the estate, and Tony's sophisticated taste: he had built a very David Hockney-looking swimming pool to contrast these. But he did have a real knowledge of the country and of animals, birds and wild flowers. In the garden were aviaries of rare birds from all over the world and the house was always decorated with imaginative flower arrangements. At this time Tony was married to Vanessa Redgrave, but neither she nor the children joined us; instead there were young men of various nationalities, rather like courtiers, fulfilling his every whim. There were also a great many greyhounds.

We took turns to do the cooking. We would all eat together, including the ladies who came to do the cleaning, at a long trestle table under the trees, overlooking the waterfall and olive groves. One day I was the cook and had made a huge beef casserole, full of herbs, vegetables, wine and, I think, even brandy. The kitchen was the best room in the house to my mind and was wonderfully equipped. I felt proud of my casserole and it was a success – lunch was going very well. The plates were cleared and Tony appeared with a magnificent chocolate gâteau, simply huge, that he had made. 'Ungela must have the first piece.' (His 'A's' were always 'U's': Tony was the originator of the sloppy, Royal Court way of talking, the Royal Court accent.) I graciously accepted the cake and cut the damned thing. What he'd put in it I don't know but it was something that made me very high. I'm not sure how long it was before I felt terribly ill and totally barmy. Irrationality took hold. I seized quite a small branch from a nearby tree and tried to pull it over me, announcing that I must hide under this vast, dark bough. Finally, a doctor had to be found, who gave me an injection which relieved the house party of my insane ravings for over twenty-four hours. I came round ashamed of myself but furious with Tony, and I remember wondering how he would face the music. But he walked into my room as soon as he heard I had come to, with his hands behind his back, the penitent schoolboy. 'Ungela, which hund will you huv?'

'Oh, both I should think.'

Both was right. He held them out for me to take from him the most lovely bunches of wild flowers I have ever seen. I forgave him at once, of course – the many-sided, clever experimentalist, the typical product of the Royal Court Theatre.

*

I remember on one occasion being with Robert Morley at Le Touquet on my own, Robin having gone back to England ahead of me, and we made friends in the Casino with a shipping tycoon and a very 'got-up', rather gushing lady who was his friend for the weekend. The men turned to serious gambling; she and I repaired to the bar together, where we shared a bottle of champagne. She leant across the table and, very *sotto voce*, said, 'May I ask you something very personal?'

Intrigued, I replied, 'Nothing I would like more.'

'Tell me,' she continued, 'and please don't think me indelicate. Do you, I mean, do you ever meet Mrs Morley?'

I entered into the spirit of things and said, in a low voice, 'I do confess I have met her very often and am sometimes included in family events.'

As Joan and I were constantly together in the jolliest possible circumstances, I thought this answer correct on all points. The

Pempey (Penelope Dudley Ward) and me

Mr Sco in the garden at Cuckfield

The dancing grin (Robin left, and above, James, Edward and Robert)

Edward with daughter Lucy

Emilia Fox: Samson would have been pleased

mysterious lady then said how she envied me: devoted though she was to the friend with whom she was enjoying this weekend, she apparently was not as fortunate as I in that particular respect.

The following morning Robert and I were at the airport. He always took immense and wicked pleasure in the fact that I shook with terror whenever I was about to fly in an aeroplane. During the dreadful wait in the airport lounge, the mysterious lady of the Casino bore down upon us. She was dressed in a long white cloak, with yards of chiffon wound round her head, the ends flying from her shoulders.

'Ah,' said she, swooping towards us, 'I have just managed to catch you. It has been such a happy meeting and I wanted so much to say a final goodbye.' We were quite overcome, but undeterred she fell on me and kissed me on both cheeks. 'Goodbye, goodbye,' she said, as our flight was called. As I was putting on my safety belt, stricken with fear, Robert Morley turned to me and said, 'You know who that strange figure was, dear one, don't you, who has just kissed you so determinedly on both cheeks? You know who she was?'

'No, I haven't the faintest idea who she was.'

'Well, dear one,' said Robert, 'it was Death!' I have no idea why this was so funny, but it was so typical of Robert.

*

Robin had been so busy working and playing that I didn't think he could have missed me. I was wrong. There was something he wished to discuss with me, urgently.

He began: 'I'm thinking of leaving MCA.'

'Why?'

'I don't like the whole philosophy; it treats human beings like cattle, only giving them shelter and water if they are making money.'

'So, if you leave, what next?'

'At least if I can't be an actor, I can be a producer. Robert Morley and Peter Ustinov want me to set up in management with them and we would call ourselves the Robin Fox Partnership.' He told me that he would sacrifice a very big pension that would have been his on retirement, had he remained at MCA. Did I mind?

'Not in the least.'

And so it was all arranged. There is no doubt that whatever role Peter Ustinov was playing he was the best company in the world, as indeed he was when he played actor-manager for a very brief period. I was often with the three of them as they wined and dined and laughed together – Peter was magically funny. He had rented a house next to Carol Reed's in the King's Road; his passions then were a pretty wife called Suzanne, fishing boats off the Goodwin Sands and motor cars. He knew a great deal about food and it was a pleasure to be his guest or his host. He could draw as wittily as he could talk – I think he was very near to being a genius.

We realized almost immediately that Peter had a natural resistance to being tied down. I never heard that harsh words were exchanged but in about three weeks he and the money that was to be invested by him were gone. So Robin had to set out on his new dream of being creative, of commissioning plays, of creating work for actors, with just Robert. Robert made all this seem very plausible, although in retrospect I think what he really wanted was to get Robin's exclusive attention. Dream it was, however. Fine actor that Robert was, experienced and professional, he lacked any of the practical nitty-gritty, common-sense temperament essential in management. He made a lot of money, he shared a lot of money generously with all who were close to him, and he had the capacity to fritter away a fortune.

For years Robert had been presented in London in plays, mostly written by himself, by H. M. Tennent. Hugh 'Binkie' Beaumont, who was then head of Tennents, was dedicated to the theatre and at that period ruling it. He was a shrewd, fascinating man, whom very few knew intimately but who was always referred to with familiarity – he was Binkie to everyone, and everyone had a very wholesome respect for him: to work for

Binkie was the prize most actors and actresses aimed at. Both Robert and Robin were devoted to Binkie and there never appeared to be a moment of ill-feeling when Robert, his biggest star, announced that in future his plays would be presented by his own management, the Robin Fox Partnership. Surely Binkie must have felt at least a touch of chagrin at the loss of his money-making star? But he, Robert and Robin remained firm friends.

The first venture of the Robin Fox Partnership was a play Robert wrote and acted in called *Six Months' Grace* at the Phoenix Theatre. His co-star was Yvonne Arnaud, and with two such stars it would have been difficult to fail. Next, a play by Ben Levy, *The Rape of the Belt*, had a good run at the Piccadilly; in the cast were not only the author's wife, Constance Cummings, but also John Clements and his enchanting, witty wife, Kay Hammond, and Richard Attenborough.

As long as Robert Morley was acting for the Company, it was difficult to go wrong, for the public loved him. Even before Robin and he were partners, we had an investment in an André Roussin comedy, *The Little Hut*, which Nancy Mitford had translated from the French and which ran for over two years; judging by the crowds that stormed the theatre on the last night when Robert was stopping for a rest and change, it could be running still. Our investment wasn't big, but it was of great help when it came to paying the bills.

Robert played for the Partnership in a musical at Drury Lane, also translated from the French, called *Fanny*. We did it with Sandor Gorlinsky, who was agent for many opera singers and conductors and found it strange to discover that Robert was tone-deaf and could not hear any tunes at all; but he spoke his numbers and gave a moving and funny performance, and was very amused at himself. On one occasion during this run I was with him when 'God Save the Queen' was played. Robert turned to me and said, 'How very civil of them, darling, to play my theme song.'

Fanny lost money. I think there was a sense of warning in the air but life in Robert's dressing-room at Drury Lane was magical. There were streams of visitors from all over the world – his hospitality was legendary. He and Ros Chatto, the Partnership's general manager, had established a tradition that at whatever theatre he was playing, a fine meal should be served between the matinée and the evening performance, and it amused him that the menus might be English, French, Spanish, Indian – each one more perfect than the last. Boulestin sent them in, Robert told me, but in fact clever Ros cooked them at home and took them to the theatre.

Towards the end of *Fanny*, our youngest son, Robert, aged five, was taken out one day from home by the Italian au pair girl, Gina, whose boyfriend wished to impress her with his prowess at golf. Demonstrating his drive, he sent the ball flying in the approved manner, hitting Robert in the temple with his follow-through, fracturing his skull and nearly killing him out-right. Barbara Evans, my woman doctor friend, was passing our house at the very moment Robert was being carried in and recognized at once that something was gravely wrong. She came in to investigate. A fairly accurate diagnosis may not have been difficult but Robert's life was saved because she telephoned her husband Philip Evans, who was by now senior physician at Great Ormond Street Hospital, and he advised that the child be brought there with all speed. This was done by Cocky Farr, who thought Robert would probably die on the journey. He ordered me into the back seat of the car and laid Robert across my knees, with the wound in his head facing downwards so that any blood would go on to the floor and not into his skull. He also stopped about every three minutes, it seemed, to take his pulse, to see if he was still alive. This stopping agitated me and perhaps it was just as well that I had no idea then of the reason.

Looking back on this journey we can laugh, because although Cocky was an inspired doctor he had absolutely no sense of direction, and got lost more than once on the way to Great Ormond Street – I sometimes think there's nothing I don't know about agonizing anxiety.

Philip Evans was waiting for us outside the hospital and so was Robin, who had been tracked down in Oxford where he had gone to see the preview of a play. Philip Evans, who once saved Robin's life, now did the same for Robin's youngest son. He had arranged for Mr Kenneth Till, a wonderful neurosurgeon, to see Robert, and after all the necessary investigations he told us he must operate. In my misery I asked him, 'Do you think he will die?'

'I don't think it's entirely unlikely,' he said, and when he saw my stricken face he was wonderfully honest, telling me that until he could ascertain the extent of Robert's injuries he really couldn't give us a definite picture. But he did say that Robert might be affected mentally and that this, perhaps, might be worse for us than facing his death.

Robin's reactions were braver than mine. He elected to remain at the hospital, as near to the door of the operating theatre as he was allowed. I ran from the scene. Where did I run? To Robert Morley in his dressing room at Drury Lane. Of course, he knew all that was happening: Robert was his godson, and he was a man who really loved children. His management of this fraught moment was typical. He was totally calm. He cooled the sense of drama by deciding to chide me about some petty matter that had nothing to do with the present. He knew me well, and knew how I would react with fury at some unjust accusation and so forget for a moment the real tension and anxiety. I behaved exactly as he knew I would, and tears of rage and annoyance with him eased the misery.

After two hours, when the curtain had been down for some time, Robin stood at the dressing-room door: the operation had been successful, the boy would live, and his brain had not been affected. I felt grateful then – and always will – to Robert. I have often fought him and argued with him, but he is a real friend who has always been near in times of personal trouble.

10

The Fox and the Grades

The Partnership had offices on the first floor of 24 Old Burlington Street, and for a time we used the comfortable flat on the floor above. Robin didn't have a room that could be called an office; he and Robert shared a charming sitting room where he could never be alone. There were lunch parties for all and sundry, which sometimes included the children of all three families, the Morleys, the Foxes and Ros Chatto's sons. Different secretaries of Ros's choice would come and go; nice girls, I remember, but if they were efficient they gave up in no time. After first nights Ros and I played hostess together for big parties at the office, and our flat upstairs was used as well. After *The Rape of the Belt*, the so-called office was turned into a casino and the croupiers were John Clements and Richard Attenborough. Too many invitations went out with no record of who had been invited, and there were so many famous names that gate-crashing must have been the order of the night: my memory of the next morning was chaos and green baize, yards and yards of it, that we had bought for the 'tables'. I was given a job: 'Take it away.' I still have rolls of the stuff in my attic. I use it to line drawers for the silver, and whenever I get out my scissors to cut it up, I remember the lunacy of that period of our lives.

I am never quite sure why we fell so deeply into the trap we did. If there was an excuse it might have been that while the wine was flowing downstairs, deep and unhappy family problems surrounded Robin as he walked to his flat on the top floor. There is no doubt that the boys wanted to be near their father. Edward's romance with Tracey Reed started here; James and Sarah Miles conducted their tempestuous affair here.

There was no lull in the Fox family dramas when Jonathan Sieff was smashed badly racing at Le Mans. Michael sent for Robin who turned his back on every problem of his own to answer this call for help. Without doubt, Jonathan owes his life to Robin, who got the right help and stayed to support Daphne and Michael through all the traumatic efforts that went into saving the boy's life. I only recall this because when Robin finally came back, the Partnership was teetering on the edge of collapse.

The crash finally came in the form of a big musical called *The Love Doctor*. With this Robin and Robert succeeded in making every mistake in the book. It was an amalgamation of three plays by Molière, one being *Le Malade Imaginaire*, set to music with fascinating and original scenery and costumes designed by Bernard Daydé. The music was by Americans who came over with an American director. The impression I gained was that the entire production was dominated by quarrels, misunderstandings, chaos and confusion. The final straw was laid on when Robert got rid of everybody else and announced that he would direct it.

The first time I was anywhere near this ill-fated production was when I was shown into my seat for the first night, wearing a most expensive dress. I thought the show very good and very glamorous, and to this day I remember it as one of the best presented musicals I have ever seen. The reception was ecstatic, and we all went in high spirits to a delicious after-show supper at a restaurant in Gerrard Street. A messenger came from Fleet Street with the early morning papers: the first reviews were excellent and spirits flew even higher. Only a few hours later, after a display of one of the more sinister mysteries of the newspaper world, the joy of success was turned into the despair of disaster. All the later notices were appalling, and with them came the demise of the Robin Fox Partnership: we were nearly bankrupt.

A pleasant surprise came next. One of the top people in the business at that time was Prince Littler, Chairman of Moss Empires and Stoll Theatres. For a couple of years Robin and I had enjoyed his personal friendship: we saw a great deal of him and his wife, Nora, in the country, dining with them often at weekends, when Robin played bridge. Nora was a charming woman, Prince a small, fat, sharp-eyed, tough man, famous for being very mean; but it was he, on hearing that we had our backs to the wall, who came spontaneously to our aid and insisted upon lending us money. He even put out one or two feelers about Robin joining his business.

At the same time Leslie Grade, brother of Lew Grade and Bernard Delfont, made a very definite offer to Robin to go into business with him as a theatrical agent once again. Leslie, who was a most successful figure in music hall, wanted to get into 'legitimate' theatre. When I heard of the Grade offer I said, 'Whatever is he offering you a job for? You had a law suit a couple of weeks ago and although you gave evidence, your side lost.' (Some highly technical case had come up in which Robin's evidence had been needed, as he was a lawyer.) Robin laughed and gave an imitation of Leslie Grade: 'I wanchya to join me, Robin. I know you lost the case – but I love the way you did it.' This was an attitude we both understood and enjoyed, so, fond as I was of Prince Littler, I never hesitated in my advice. 'Join the Grades,' I said.

Leslie Grade was born Winogradsky but he was pure Cockney, having arrived in this country as an infant. He was small and delicate-looking, with a big forehead and receding fair hair; his name didn't appear much in the papers, but he was the *éminence grise* of his remarkable family. If he'd heard me use that phrase he'd have said, 'What does that mean, Angie?' gazing at me questioningly with his large, pale, rather watery blue eyes staring, his jaw dropping down in questioning surprise. Woe betide anyone who was fooled. Perhaps the greatest surprise was that

Robin really and truly loved this little man, and this love was returned one hundred per cent. From the day the Grade Organization was formed, the work they put in together was non-stop and prodigious, but it was laughter and enjoyment all the way.

Leslie had been married twice. Michael Grade, now a distinguished man in his own right, was the child of his first marriage but when we came on the scene Leslie was very happily married to Audrey, who was not Jewish but who had adopted his religion on joining the family. The children of this marriage were Anita and Anthony. Leslie was a most loving husband and father. Lew and Bernie were also very happily married with families of their own, but the entire roost was ruled by their wonderful Jewish mama. Mrs Grade had brought the boys up in great poverty in the East End but when we met her she was the legendary mother figure, now prosperous due to her sons' hard work and to the fact that they were brilliant men. She was a handsome woman, expensively dressed, with fine furs and jewels, still ruling her boys with a rod of iron. There was still a trace of broken English in her speech – they came from Lithuania – mixed with Cockney. She was, of course, justly proud of her children and their achievements. A story was circulated that when she was presented to the Queen Mother by her son Bernie when he was front man of the Royal Command Performance at the Palladium, the Queen Mother congratulated Mrs Grade on her distinguished sons. Mrs Grade replied with a broad smile: 'Your lot haven't done so badly, either.'

All the boys were inordinately proud of their mother. Once, when Leslie and Audrey were spending the weekend with us, Leslie wanted to drive over to Eastbourne to visit his mother where she was on holiday. He didn't want to go without letting her know, so he telephoned the hotel and asked to speak to Mrs Grade.

'Mrs Grade? Mrs Grade? We have nobody of that name here.'

'Don't be silly. She's my mother and I booked the suite for her, she's my guest.'

This argument persisted for some time, the telephonist at the

Grand Hotel denying the presence of any Mrs Grade and Leslie becoming positively irate until, finally, he demanded to speak to the manager. The manager asked him to hold on while he investigated. He returned in due course to say, 'Well, sir, we do have a Mrs Grade-Delfont staying in the Hotel. Would that be the lady to whom you are referring?'

'I'm not *referring*,' bellowed Leslie. 'She's my mother!'

By this time Robin and I had got the giggles but Leslie had lost all humour and slammed down the receiver, only to pick it up at once and dial the same number again. This time he asked to be put through to Mrs Grade-Delfont. Mother answered the telephone to hear 'Wotchya playing at, Mother? Wotchya doin' to me? I been looking for you. I couldn't find you. What is this Mrs Grade-Delfont?'

Mother was quite unmoved. 'Well, Leslie, I wanted them to know that *all* my sons are doing well.'

Family life for the Grades was lived at that pitch.

*

Robin moved into offices in the building Leslie's firm occupied in Regent Street. He and Leslie soon started a pattern, which Robin already knew well, of buying a lot of the big agencies but always leaving them absolutely free to continue working under their own names and interfering as little as possible, except to enable them to use and be useful to nearly all the big stars in the business. Our life changed abruptly. Money started to roll in on Robin's side, as it had for Leslie for a long time. We couldn't buy off our personal problems, of course, but materially we were suddenly better off. Leslie was a generous man and Robin was a workaholic. In my usual, unbusinesslike way, I have no idea what Robin's salary was but from the very beginning it must have been substantial, as we were able to pay back Prince Littler's generosity immediately and in full.

We gave up the offices in Old Burlington Street though Stillwell Derby, our landlords, allowed us to keep the flat until we had found somewhere else, which was my task. I was in my element and in no time the Fox address was 12 Eaton Square. We had a ground-floor flat: the drawing room led out into a garden. For the first time in my life the chauffeur was at the door in a new Mercedes – only a short time before, I used to wonder if I had the fare for the bus or the underground. The flat was very attractive and big enough to be used for all the entertaining which Robin and I so enjoyed extending to the people he worked for.

The person who benefited most from this remarkable set-up was our youngest son, Robert: he met Leslie when he was an adolescent boy and from the first moment loved him as much as we did. Robert was now at Harrow. He had a greater capacity for work than his brothers, at school anyway, and showed signs of being a classicist; we were even told that if he worked he would get into a university with ease. He got good O and A Level results but being full of rebellion and dislike for the school left Harrow very young. Very soon he took the first steps towards a career in the theatre. I recall a last, vivid picture I have of his time at Harrow: I went on my own to see him play cricket. It was his father he had wanted, of course, but Robin told me firmly and pompously that he had an important business appointment in London he must keep. Tim Warr was then housemaster of Rendell's, Robert's house, and seeing that I was bored he invited me to the house for tea, saying, 'There's a marvellous match on at Wimbledon at the moment – we should get a glimpse of it on television.' It was a marvellous match. The cameras went, of course, to the Royal Box, and there was Wimbledon's Royal Patron, Princess Marina, Duchess of Kent; and the good-looking man sitting next to her was Robin Fox. Thus did I learn of his friendship with this elegant Royal lady. This time, for a change, I was the last woman in London to know.

Robert would spend hours in Leslie Grade's office – I'm not quite sure why, but he picked up the tag of 'Rocky Joe Ten Per Cent' and that has remained his nickname. He learned much from Leslie and could have had no finer teacher. He is now himself a successful producer. Michael White started him off, and he went into the Duke Street office, first to look after Paul Scofield, who was then playing in *Savages*. Soon he was managing the office, then became Michael's associate producer on *Chorus Line* and *Annie*, with his wife Celestia casting the latter. With Michael's friendship and blessing – they are alike in some ways – he left and set up on his own, producing, to begin with, *Anyone for Dennis?* by John Wells and later *Another Country* by Julian Mitchell which he has just filmed. He is a passionate believer in the commercial theatre and thinks it is up to people like him to get the money and make it successful. I see the best of his father and Leslie Grade in his attitudes to people who work with him and for him.

*

With Leslie and Robin the Grade Organization really started to flourish: clients that Robin had lost through going into management returned to his fold and they were so successful in the world of music hall and the legitimate theatre that they thought it would be great fun to go into films – everything was fun, what a tonic! This is how our business should be, and anyone who loses this feeling should get out.

Leslie was responsible for Cliff Richard and the Shadows, and we made two highly profitable films with them, *Summer Holiday* and *The Young Ones*. Cliff, Leslie's protégé, came to the theatre with us one night; my memory is of a nice and unaffected boy. They also made *Sparrows Can't Sing*, adapted from a successful Joan Littlewood production. We held the première at a cinema in the East End, not only because that had been where Leslie, Lew and Bernie had lived, but also because Robin had great admiration for Joan Littlewood's work at the Theatre Royal, Stratford East.

Robin and Leslie started looking round for something a little more serious. Joe Losey, the American director, was very anxious to make a film of *The Servant* by Robin Maugham, nephew of

Somerset Maugham, and Dirk Bogarde was keen to play the main role. Everything hinged on two things: getting the finances – always a big first – and finding a suitable young man to be corrupted by the character Dirk would play.

Very casually, Robin said would they like to see his son, James, who since he came out of the Coldstream Guards had attended the Central School of Speech and Drama and had played a few parts on the stage, though his only recent film experience had been a small part in Tony Richardson's *The Loneliness of the Long Distance Runner*. The moment Joe Losey and Dirk Bogarde saw James, he was the only actor they wanted to play the part; it wouldn't have mattered whose son he was. Robin became his agent. They were fairly certain that the picture wouldn't make money, and James was paid a very small salary, though finally Leslie decided that he himself would be responsible for the finance. Robin loved Joe Losey, and it would be difficult to find words that fully express the help and encouragement this great professional gave to an unknown actor called James Fox. They even had his girlfriend, Sarah Miles, in the picture, and very good she was too.

In the nursery Sarah would have been called a 'handful' – mischievous but very lovable, a child who very early on learned to get round everybody and have her own way. As she grew up, she developed enough sex appeal to rock any boat. James was under her spell for a number of years. An incident that happened one day illustrated her carefree sang-froid. I had become a keen gardener and one year grew all my own annuals from seed. Only gardeners will know the labour involved – sowing, pricking out and finally, with hours of labour, planting out. I wanted the front garden at Cuckfield to be a blaze of colour. Hundreds of tiny plants were finally ready and planting them took several days. As I was finishing I stood up, stretched my aching back. Sarah and Addo, her huge white wolfhound, arrived at the gate. Sarah took off Addo's lead. 'There you are, my darling,' she said, 'now you can have a lovely time.' She was so right: it took the white beauty less than half a minute to rake up with his huge paws what seemed like every annual I had loved from birth, and scatter earth and confusion over my creation, as well as relieving himself well and truly after a long journey.

The Servant brought about my first meeting with Dirk Bogarde, who became a client of Robin's as well as the closest possible friend to us both. They shot the film in Royal Avenue, Chelsea on a very small budget, and when Joe Losey had finished he invited me to a private showing. I reacted not as an ordinary member of an audience but very subjectively – as an appalled and outraged mother. That anyone should see my son as a weak and degenerate playboy who could be defeated by an evil servant! Leaving the cinema in Wardour Street I was in such a rage that I kicked a dustbin very hard and broke my toe, and ever since have been a bore to people trying to fit me with a right shoe. When Joe telephoned Robin that evening on quite another matter, I seized the telephone – something I would never normally do – and abused Joe in a most hysterical manner for painting my son in this way, although, of course, even *I* knew it had been a good performance. Joe had a low, guttural voice with a mid-Western accent. I can hear him saying now, in his slow, laconic way, 'You're just being stupid. That's the guy he is.'

The film was a huge success for all concerned: it made James a big star and he went on to do many more pictures, though none, with the possible exception of *King Rat*, in which I thought he was magnificent, came anywhere near *The Servant*. Huge success, a great deal of money, fame, and all the pressure and publicity that go with them did destroy him temporarily, and for a time he bore out Joe's observant insight. The person perhaps even more bewildered, unhappy, and forlorn was the star's mother, who showed a unique lack of understanding.

*

I knew the other Grade brothers too; Bernie not quite so well but I found him tremendous fun. Once we found ourselves on a holiday with Lew – Robin, our son Robert and myself, at Juan

Les Pins. Lew announced that he would come to the beach and sunbathe with us; this meant that as well as sporting his enormous cigar, he would put on a yachting cap and pull it down over his eyes as far as it would go. He would then huddle in a deck-chair, swathing himself in as many blankets, rugs or towels as he could muster by snatching them from the rest of the party. Thus he would remain all day. When we visited restaurants in the evening, at which he always played host, he would give graphic descriptions of the glorious day he had enjoyed in the sun.

Even wrapped up like this and feigning sleep – feigned it was, for cigar smoke emanated in waves from the blanketed figure – he would never miss a detail of what was said. His wife, Kathy, an extremely pretty blonde, used to discuss her make-up and what she used for her exquisite complexion. I remarked that I would go shopping that afternoon and buy some of the same. In a few minutes Lew stirred and, refusing all offers of help, said he must slip back to the hotel to fetch something. In about half an hour he returned with a springing step and a joyful air, still smoking his cigar, with his chin resting on a pile of glamorous-looking parcels: he had been to the beauty shop and bought me every single thing he had heard Kathy and me discuss.

That was one of the sides of the real Lew Grade; another was less endearing. Robin, with his wily brain and ceaseless application, clinched an enormous deal for something Lew wanted more than anything in the world. Negotiations with another company, EMI, had been long and arduous and there was some sticking point. We were at Michael Grade's first wedding at the Dorchester after the ceremony, all of us, including the bride and groom, enjoying an extravagant ball. Robin and I were sitting with the chairman of Lex Garage, Mr Chinn, his wife and their son, Trevor; the other people at the table were dancing. Robin looked across the room to Sir Joseph Lockwood, chairman of EMI, and he suddenly said to me, 'My God, I've got it. I'm off to have a word with Joe Lockwood; expect me when you see me.' He wasn't very long, but I looked across to their table several times and saw them deep in conversation.

Suddenly Robin got up. He came first to me and almost shouted, 'I've done it! We've got it!' Then he went straight across to Lew at the top table. Immediately it was as if a great balloon had gone up, or a happy air-ship. Lew jumped to his feet like an excited child and yelled boisterously for more champagne.

Joseph Lockwood came over to the table where I, by now, had been summoned: tremendous toasts were drunk by him and by the Grades for what Robin had done. He would 'get at least £50,000 for himself'. This was a spontaneous gesture. Robin was made a director of EMI but while Leslie was alive he never took the promised £50,000: he had the view that, given a few years, it would perhaps be possible to have money abroad, and that he and I would buy, even build, a tiny house in France. When Leslie had a cerebral haemorrhage, which ended his and Robin's partnership, we thought it might be more difficult getting the money but Robin never doubted for a moment that he would have it when he needed it. He had such trust in his friends. When it was Robin's turn to become fatally ill and then to die, I don't think I even had a letter from Lew, though had I asked for the money I know it would have been forthcoming.

*

There were times when Robert Morley could be such a wise, magnanimous, really good friend. One of these occasions was when we were with the Duc di Sangro whose house we were occupying in Italy at Ravello when Robert was making *Beat the Devil* for John Huston. My Italian being non-existent, I thought I could help the Duc, who couldn't make out who anybody was, by shouting very loudly, enunciating very clearly and explaining those present in far too much detail. Robert must have done something unusually nice that morning and I screamed at the Duc, 'He is a saint, you see, a saint. Aren't you?' I said, turning to Robert.

Robert was delighted. 'I know that, my dear. What are you going to call me?'

'St Mor,' I replied.

'Absolutely right, my dear, and as you know, I always think of you as one of the Walter-Mitty-Foxes.'

These two names stuck to us for many years and we enjoyed the joke. I can't say the same for the Duc di Sangro, who was utterly confused, but no doubt grateful for the money the film company were paying to house lunatics in his beautiful home.

In order to reach Ravello for *Beat the Devil*, Robin and I had set out with Robert one wicked winter's day in a motor driven by Robert's chauffeur. Record ice and snow delayed us, and we were held up and very late. Things were so bad that Robert said he wanted to stop off at the Carlton Hotel in Cannes and do a little gambling – a further twenty-four hours off the map could make no difference. We arrived in Cannes, booked in without difficulty at the Carlton and were soon sprawled on the beds in Robin's and my bedroom as Robert wanted to telephone Joan and he always liked an audience. He seized the telephone. He wanted to let her know that he had arrived safely and not to believe anything she may have read in the newspapers. He was safe and sound and well. Joan has a very loud voice and it was immediately clear that she hadn't given him a thought, let alone read the newspapers.

Robert was co-starring in *Beat the Devil* with Gina Lollabrigida and Humphrey Bogart and a further list of international stars and near-stars stretching from Ravello to Timbuctoo. When we arrived at this dotty, fairyland scene, we were greeted by the production manager, a penniless Italian prince, Prince Alessandra di Tasca. Full of charm, he walked us to the Duc di Sangro's house. He did hope it was good enough and that Signora Fox would enjoy running it. It was good enough. It was magnificent, the main villa in this show-place village, where Mussolini had entertained Hitler. As for my having to run it, there were armies of servants who had lived there for many years with their entire families hidden in the servants' quarters below stairs; the Duc, I learned, appeared but rarely and never realized his own bounty.

The day we arrived hundreds of villagers and extras brought

up from Naples had been hired to scream under the star's window 'Viva Gina Lollabrigida'. Robert Morley soon put this to rights. The following morning we were awakened by crowds below our window yelling 'Viva Roberto Morley, il grande attore Inglese'. Quite right, we thought, and have loved this joke ever since. A few doors away the main hotel housed the director, John Huston, the author, Truman Capote, Guillaume, the hairdresser from Paris and hordes of comers and goers, famous and not-so-famous. John Huston is the most brilliant, arrogant and detached man I have ever met. Truman Capote might have been brilliant but he was dotty. He had no script ready at all, although the crew and stars were ready to shoot. I remember he had a bird, a real bird in a cage in Rome, to whom he must telephone for hours every day because (a) the bird liked him to and (b) it was helping him with his script. It was soon clear the bird was not doing well enough. No script turned up and everyone wrote a bit on scraps of paper, and on their cuffs, at times, which John Huston screened somehow. (The film was hugely successful, so there must be a lesson to be learned from this method, or lack of it.)

Jennifer Jones, then married to David Selznik, was having a nervous breakdown because one of her previous husbands – the father of her two boys – had recently committed suicide. Givenchy had brought trunks of white toile as bases for her dresses and just managed to fit some of these, but Jennifer would do no more, she just couldn't, so Givenchy – a great man of the world – simply draped her in toile and the critics wrote of the brilliance of Givenchy dressing this exquisite woman entirely in white. Brilliant he was – and very, very patient.

Humphrey Bogart provided the tragedy in this lunatic scene. He was dying of cancer. Between 'takes' he sat morosely in his caravan, quiet and dignified and ill – no fuss, a real professional to the end. I never met him, never spoke to him, but I shall remember always the sad, ill eyes, wearily watching the charade. The last time I ever saw him was when Robert and I were driving away from Ravello, full of joy at leaving. Humphrey Bogart was on the back of a donkey, loping across the village square, a real Don Quixote.

Film stars have one thing in common with royalty: you never get to know them nor they you – there is no time. I played ping-pong often with Gina Lollabrigida betwen scenes. She would take off that hideous wig with relief – she was such a pretty woman with a wonderful figure like a young girl – and we would play in earnest, without a single laugh. I tried sincerely to help the distraught Jennifer Jones; I failed one hundred per cent there as well. I only ever saw David Selznik as an exasperated, indeed defeated, husband, never as a great Hollywood mogul. Orson Welles was not in the film, but he would turn up from time to time and watch mischievously.

Amalfi and the sea were right below us but John Huston made all the technicians recreate a harbour high in the hills in Ravello, a mountain village. Each night he and his consortium at the hotel a few doors from us drank themselves silly and Guillaume would do the men's hair. Truman Capote became the platinum blond we all got used to in photographs; huge, grey John Huston had a 'perm'. So Boy George is not an original. Huston one night was drunkenly smoking in bed when the sheets caught fire. He doused the flames with gin and that was very nearly the end of an Eminent American Film Director! What a relief it was to leave.

*

During that briefest of stopovers at Cannes on the way to Ravello, I had encountered Frederick Lonsdale in the lift: Freddy, my natural father, whom I hadn't seen for years. He was living at the Carlton, alone. Robert was entranced by this meeting and immediately asked Freddy to dine with us; he refused. I remember pacing the room with childish tears very near the surface. Even now I'm glad I hadn't shown my feelings since almost immediately the telephone rang, and Freddy invited *us* to dine with *him*. I learned that night that he was a very good host, and an amusing and stimulating man. I learned too that he was well read and intelligent, more serious, more thoughtful than my mother – my only informant – had told me. We went to the Casino after dinner. Like him, I never gambled, so we sat in the bar and talked a bit, impersonally, and drank a little too much. It was a lifelong habit of his that he drank only champagne, and this had to be decanted into a jug. I asked him to write yet another play; he told me, fairly sharply, not to be a fool. No one, he said, wanted any more to hear his views or share his values ever again. The following day all he and I exchanged were hello and goodbye. We never met again. I liked him very much indeed – I always shall – and I shall, with good reason, wonder why.

11
Edward and James

Edward always gave us surprises. Twice he had nearly died in his first few months and twice he surprised us by living. He then saved up his surprises until he was just past adolescence. In fact, he lulled those nearest to him into a positively smug acceptance that he was a quiet, sensitive boy, with an amateurish talent for the piano. He loathed going back to school but then who doesn't? He made no sound but looked stricken and anguished, particularly on returning to Harrow.

When I had to make a decision to enter him, and later James, without their father to share in this decision, I never doubted for a single moment they must go to Harrow. Robin had been there and so had their grandfather and uncle on my mother's side. Soccer was the game that was played there, and that was unusual: Grandpapa Morice had later played for England.

Shall I ever forgive myself for making Edward go? Was he unhappy, though he never said so? Yes, very. He was a very good boy, something always worrying to those in charge. After about two terms the Matron asked to see me. 'If only he would do something tiresome or naughty, I should feel he was normal. It's all most worrying.' She should have been with him five years later; it might have reassured her.

His housemaster had been a fellow pupil with Robin and they were on excellent terms, but he was incapable of any real communication with the boys or their parents. Once, when

Edward told us that the rainwater was pouring in on his bed, rather reluctantly Robin thought he ought to look into this assertion, and took the housemaster with him. To his irritation, Robin saw Edward had been speaking the truth, so he remonstrated: 'This really is too bad. I want you to have something done about it at once.'

'Oh,' said the housemaster, 'I think you're making rather a fuss. It's only running on his legs.'

Years later, when my youngest son, Robert, was at Harrow, I took Simone Signoret along for a visit and this darling Left-winger called me the most evil, cruel woman she had ever met for leaving such a sweet boy in such a hell-hole. Paying those fees with great difficulty, I suppose, made us feel we must be getting something back.

Edward did get as far as being a prefect. I think I'm correct in saying this entitled him to ride a bicycle. Both Edward and James were good at games. Edward was a loner, but he did play squash and racquets for the school and became a very good swimmer. A quirk in his makeup meant that he lost interest the moment he became first-class at any game. He would go all out to win the prize, the cherished Cup, and then not play seriously again. The competitive urge vanished but he still plays for fun and enjoys real tennis. James was a wicked, charming rebel. He played fives for the school and won the Rattigan Prize for play-writing. They got a few 'O' Levels between them; Robin and I thought that quite funny. It didn't worry us in the least that their results were so unimpressive.

James was befriended by a wonderful teacher, although he was never up to him, the distinguished classics master, E. V. C. Plumptre. We heard James was continually visiting Plumptre, and even his father thought he had better look into the reasons for such an unlikely relationship. We got ourselves invited for lunch and so started on a friendship enjoyed by all the family. 'Plum' was an intellectual, scholarly man, very sensitive and shy, with little that was masculine about him. He was a very nice man, a totally good influence on James and, in the difficult years that were to follow school, he was a help and calm comfort to me when we were both baffled and saddened at the turn James's life had taken. In Plum's last term at Harrow, his pupils got eight open scholarships to Oxford and Cambridge. He told me that all these scholarships had done was to help his pupils to get a foot in a door that would cast a thin shaft of light which they could try to follow. When he retired Plum bought a pretty house at Herstmonceaux, because a grateful mother of a pupil had given him a present of money in her lifetime rather than leaving it in her will, so that she could see him enjoy it. Later, he moved to Eastbourne and I saw him at least once a month until he died. He was the good side of Harrow whilst Edward and James were there. Plum had something else besides scholarship and learning and that was his beloved Scottish housekeeper, Margaret Rose. She helped to make the food and the fun in his home at Harrow a legend, and she continued this in his retirement. At Harrow she took the place Alice filled at home for James; he had been the child closest to Alice.

After Harrow came National Service. From now on, surprises all the way. Edward did well at Pirbright and with the influence of my brother-in-law, Richard Crichton, he got into the Coldstream Guards. He was the blue-eyed boy, even putting down some rather subversive event, which won him praise. He went to Eaton Hall to become an officer, but here the rot began to set in.

Edward amused his father, who totally agreed with him, by insisting that those in charge were idiots who couldn't have earned their living any other way. However, his father made it quite clear that the greater part of life is spent working with idiots; Eaton Hall would give him the experience to cope with this unhappy fact. Of course, his father was right, his advice was sound: Edward was there to learn self-discipline. He chose a harder route to learn his lesson, becoming furious and resentful, unable to take what he thought to be the totally absurd orders yelled at him and his friends. He assured his fellow sufferers that he would throw the Commanding Officer in the river, and did exactly that. Goodbye to the Coldstream Guards.

He then transferred to the Loyal Regiment, and here the going got really rough. He was now a subaltern, so there were orders to be given and responsibilities to be accepted. There was a need to have the respect and co-operation of the non-commissioned officers. Unfortunately Edward was seen as a privileged upstart who hadn't been good enough for the Coldstream Guards and nobody likes to be patronized by what is thought of as second-best. I remember the telephone call Edward made when he lost confidence. I became a distraught, worried mother, a useless role if ever there was one. Robin was more relaxed. He told Edward, 'You've got to win, and to resolve the problem by yourself. No one can do it for you. You can try getting round the men with the Fox charm, but the chances of doing any good with that are minimal. You have to establish that you are an officer with good and tried soldiers: there are no flies on them.' Edward still thought he would never be able to command this formidable group. Laughingly, Robin told him, 'Get tough. Try fear. The dice are loaded in your favour – you're the officer and finally they have to accept this.'

After his long and distinguished army service Robin's advice was worth having. Edward took it, discarding the so-called Fox charm; he then had two successful, even happy, years with the Loyal Regiment, and ever since his family have affectionately called him 'Fear' Fox.

When his National Service ended in 1957, Edward went to see his godfather, Marcus, now Lord Sieff, chairman of Marks & Spencer, and asked if he could join the firm, knowing full well that he would have to join as the lowest form of life. Marcus gave Edward a lot of his time and did his best to persuade him to take a break first, to travel and have fun – and then he might join Marks & Spencer. Edward was adamant: he wanted to join M & S then and there, and so he did.

Surprises again: he was a disaster. He hated everything to do with the work and was as rebellious as he had been at Eaton Hall. He simply didn't like the rules of the game. High on this list was the subject of clothes. He was told that on the floor he must wear a conventional dark suit, like all the other young men. As he was at the Brighton store he lived in Sussex with me. Daily I saw him leave for work in rather exaggerated country gentleman's tweeds that had once belonged to my sister's husband, whom Edward had thought very elegant. They were totally unsuitable for a member of the staff at Marks & Spencer and one Saturday the manager told him so. Edward gave in his notice. Marcus roared with laughter and said, 'Thank God, we were going to have to sack him anyway.' The best part of this episode is that Edward and Marcus enjoy to this day a most affectionate friendship.

When Edward was at home during his Marks & Spencer foray, he was white-faced, silent and deeply unhappy, impossible to communicate with at all. As I never have been a mother who could say, 'Take your moods elsewhere', I turned to our family doctor, Cocky, for advice.

'Ask him if he wants to be an actor!' he suggested. This enraged me because of course I knew it was the last thing that could have entered Edward's mind. His brother James had by now renewed his childhood stardom, enjoying huge success in *The Servant* and Edward appeared not even to notice. I was rude to Cocky who, knowing me so well, was unabashed. 'Just ask him casually. Appear to be sewing; just throw the question in a detached way.' I did. More surprise. This shy, sensitive, introverted, difficult young man did want to be an actor. Oh dear!

Robin and I were stunned. Everyone seemed to turn to Robin for advice but this time Robin turned to someone else, Glen Byam Shaw, the great director of theatre and opera. Glen was clear-sighted and a great help: he asked Robin if Edward was dedicated and physically strong. Robin knew he was certainly the second of these things. Then Glen said, 'If Edward gets into RADA, support him through that, and then don't give him a penny. He will only finally get work if driven by an absolute need to do so.'

Edward, again to our surprise, did get into RADA and when

he left we took Glen's advice. I think I can say it made him, but also it very, very nearly destroyed him.

James was having his affair with Sarah Miles. I see now that Edward was determined not to be outdone, so he fell in love, deeply, seriously, no doubt about it, no play-acting – In Love – and the object of his passion was a fellow student, Tracey Reed. She had been born Tracey Pelissier. Her mother was Penelope ('Pempey') Dudley-Ward and her grandmother was Freda Dudley-Ward who had been for so many years the mistress of and a good influence over the Prince of Wales. Later, much later, these women, particularly Freda, were to be of the greatest assistance to Edward when he came to make the television series of *Edward VIII and Mrs Simpson.* Tracey's father was Anthony Pellisier, son of Fay Compton, the actress, and nephew of Compton Mackenzie. Anthony and 'Pempey' had married in the war and divorced very soon afterwards. Pempey then married Carol Reed, the wonderful director and natural son of Beerbohm Tree, and Tracey was given his name. I don't think Anthony protested. He and I have been best friends since we were eighteen – we still are. He makes rather a habit of marrying: I always refer to him as 'more married against than married'.

Tracey at seventeen was, of her type, the most beautiful girl I have ever seen: she could wear clothes so well she appeared to have been born with elegance; she was vivacious, generous and quite impossible. Edward adored her. So did a lot of other men and it was never difficult to see why: she was a lovely girl and could be marvellous company. I'm not sure she'd had love, the right sort of love, because her mother and stepfather spoiled her materially and gave in to her over everything. Tracey had a half-brother, Max, and possibly Pempey and Carol gave him the best of themselves. Tracey's life had been run by a doting nanny.

Still, Tracey and I have been friends since the day we met. Apart from one big disagreement concerning my granddaughter, Lucy, when she was a baby, nothing has altered this. I am very fortunate to know, as very few people do, what a courageous woman and loyal friend she can be. I remember once Robin said wearily to me, 'Why the hell do both our sons have to choose destroyers?' Destroyers they were, but curiously, to Robin and to me both these strange girls were and are friendly, kind and generous in what they do and in what they say; both make me glad I'm not a man.

In no time at all Tracey was pregnant. Pempey and I, who had known each other as children at Sandwich and not met since, realized that we must meet to say, 'Where do we go from here?' I dreaded this meeting. I thought Pempey had every reason to be angry with Edward: Tracey was only seventeen. But my fears were groundless. She came to the country, was unhappy for the young ones but ready to help, if help she could. They told us they wanted an abortion arranged – not too easy twenty-three years ago. I knew an abortionist and Pempey said she had the money. What a team we made, and the matter was arranged.

I happened to walk through the hall of my house on the day prior to the abortion, and found Edward and Tracey holding hands and both in tears. I have an impulsive, spontaneous temperament and I went straight in to bat. 'So, you don't want to have an abortion!' Relief enveloped them. 'No, we don't.' I bicycled to Haywards Heath Registry Office, paid for a Special Licence and the marriage took place. There was just time to arrange a lunch with Carol, Pempey, Max, my family, Philip Evans and his wife Barbara, and Cocky. Six months later my darling granddaughter, Lucy, was born, and I have been against abortion ever since. Lucy is the best advertisement for a difficult marriage and divorce. She is a beautiful, uncomplicated girl, affectionate and very amusing and, despite the intense difficulties in her parents' marriage and their parting, appears untouched and remains devoted to them both.

*

But I am writing about Edward and what happened to him, and not the why of him. I refuse to believe we know our children, any more than they know their parents.

Edward and Tracey remained together up to the birth of Lucy in the local Cuckfield Hospital. They wanted very naturally and normally to be left on their own with the baby to make their own lives. But here the Dudley-Ward side stepped in. Tracey's old nanny was reinstated, with a large salary paid by Pempey. Tracey was – I insist on this – a born mother. She adored the child, could handle her with ease and assurance, and feed her with no difficulty whatsoever. But Pempey and Freda and Nanny descended on an idyllic scene and stopped Tracey feeding Lucy herself: 'Women of our class don't do that.' They sneered at the village hospital. It was a good hospital with a very fine maternity wing. 'What a ghastly thought,' said Freda, 'that my great-grandchild should be born in such an institution.' They were so old-fashioned and so patronizing that I had to remind myself it's better to laugh than cry.

As soon as Lucy was born, in April 1960, they bought Tracey a charming house in Little Venice. Gone was Edward and Tracey's dream of earning a place that belonged to them both. Nanny took over Lucy entirely. Tracey soon grew bored, Edward utterly miserable. He seemed to exist nowhere in this scheme of things, and inevitably Tracey turned to other men for solace. I kept remembering that just before the wedding, when Edward was so determined to go through with it despite older and wiser people promising a different solution, he had shouted in rage: 'I want for once to show that I can achieve the best. I'll do it by marrying the most beautiful girl of them all.' He did, and he paid a big price, in caring and in unhappiness, though that was shared, as it had to be, by all his family.

But it's the next surprise – and it was a surprise – that I like best of all: he started to work again, in touring companies and any repertory company that would take him. I remember turning up to see him in a leading part in *She Stoops to Conquer* at Croydon. I thought his performance was quite awful and was telling Wilfrid Hyde-White about it: 'Wilfrid, he was very bad.'

'How bad, my dear?'

'Well, appalling, Wilfrid, appalling.'

'Well, dear, if he was so bad then there's hope for him.'

Wise old Wilfrid. I didn't believe him then but I count myself lucky to see how right he was. By sheer hard work Edward has become a very good actor, after a life lived always in and around the theatre. I know for certain that it is hard work that makes an actor. Talent is not enough. Learning the hard way must have been especially rough for Edward, as James was the exception who proved the rule. In their twenties, while Edward was often out of work – among other things, he drove a van for Jaegers for eleven pounds a week – James, without enormous effort, had become a film star.

A successful younger brother is perhaps a greater challenge than the reverse; also Robin was preoccupied with James at that time. Edward received little encouragement but learned about acting wherever and however he could. He was in repertory in Dundee, where Anthony Page, Nicol Williamson and Glenda Jackson, among others, were setting forth. Robin and I went to Ipswich to see him in *Five Finger Exercise*; I remember his performance but not that we praised or encouraged him much. I also have a vivid picture of visiting him in Coventry, of the dreary atmosphere, the ugliness of the theatre, of the squalor and dirt; but I cannot recollect the play, let alone Edward's part in it. All I noticed was how much standards in the provincial theatres had deteriorated since I had toured.

While James went from film to film, earning a great deal of money, Edward slogged away, always learning: but the two of them remained very close and shared a beastly flat off Marylebone High Street. Edward's hard grind finally started to pay off and he became better known; now some parts in films came his way. Dickie Attenborough was among the first directors to use him and he has remained a constant friend over the years.

Edward may appear from all this as a long-suffering goodie, but that is not so, by a long chalk. In work he is totally reliable, but in private life I have given up taking his eccentricities seriously: it wastes energy to do so. It's not really important, just irritating, that if he's coming to lunch we may – or indeed may not – see him at tea time. Sometimes the surpriser is surprised, however. Once, when he was working at Ipswich, Edward thought he would spend the morning of a matinée day sailing on the River Deben. Generally good at sports as he was, he knew as much about sailing as a jellyfish would about mountaineering. The companions for this relaxed morning asked, 'Sail where, Ed?'

'Oh, there and back,' was the very informed answer.

Well, 'there' was all in order; as for 'and back', he hadn't reckoned on Nature. All wind subsided. Anything depending on it ceased to move. The boat was quite, quite still and would not budge, no matter what orders 'Fear' Fox shouted at it. Immense struggles saw the boat beached on a mud flat. Time to turn up at the theatre for the matinée grew near for any conscientious actor, so Edward decided to walk to the car. He plunged into thick, black mud and on reaching the river bank was in full, slimy armour. Somehow he got to his car and did make the theatre on time – but he never told me whether he changed into costume or whether the punctilious eccentric had to enter as he was in order not to let anybody down.

Edward's first really good opportunity came in television, in Henry James's *Portrait of a Lady*. I still think of this as one of the best serials, and that in it Richard Chamberlain and Edward Fox are not easily forgotten. Then in 1970 came a real break, Joe Losey's *The Go-Between*: not a big part – Lord Trimmingham – but appreciated equally in the profession and by the public. Fred Zimmerman saw the film and cast Edward in *The Day of the Jackal*. I find fascinating the deep powers of observation possessed by top film directors: Joe Losey had observed a side of James that I had no knowledge of whatsoever, and he was right; and it took Fred to see the Jackal in Edward. Now, in his films, Edward could make use of all the early training he'd received in country pursuits from Flick Fairfax-Ross. For the role of the Jackal, he knew that immense pains had to be put into the job of learning to be a good shot and more recently, making *The Shooting Party*, he was irritated by the fact that the scenes when they were out with guns were not authentic.

*

We flew over vast mountains and dark ravines to swoop down on cardboard Hollywood. It was around 4 a.m. our time. Jimmy Woolf had sent his chauffeur, who said we must hurry because Mr Jimmy was giving a dinner party to welcome us and he had told the guests 8.30 for 9 p.m. Going at great speed, all I can remember were a number of down-at-heel and empty buildings, noticeable in the gaudy glitter of the street lighting.

'What are those buildings?'

'Oh, Senator Goldwater's headquarters.'

They were tatty and dirty and derelict. He had just failed to become President of the United States.

Jimmy welcomed us. He was in Hollywood to supervise the making of *King Rat*, directed by Bryan Forbes, in which James was starring with George Segal. We must quickly unpack and change. James was there already; he ran our baths and above the noise of running water we shouted him news of home.

Into Hollywood at the deep end: at dinner Jimmy put George Cukor on my right, Warren Beatty on my left. Beautiful, now dead, Natalie Wood was at the table; so was Mike Frankovitch, head of Twentieth Century Fox Studios. The surprise couple were Professor Trevor-Roper (now Lord Dacre) and his wife. James, as the son of the visitors for whom the party was being given, was moved from table to table. Politics were the main topic. Robin and I must have got our second wind; the party seemed to go on for ever but we stayed the course.

George Cukor was the only one there who became a lasting friend. We went to his big, lonely house, full of Impressionist paintings. One day I was admiring them and I put my hand quite near a beautiful Renoir. George let out a shriek. 'Don't touch it! Don't touch it! You'll set off the alarm!' Had I done so, apparently the entire Los Angeles police force would have arrived. What price success! I had a glimpse of a swimming pool through the trees in his garden and saw some young men sunbathing by the water. They remained simply figures by the water; we were never introduced to them. Katharine Hepburn and Spencer Tracy had a small house in the grounds but we did not see them.

On Sunday around Jimmy's pool all the beautiful young people collected, many of them to get a square meal, better still a job, for which it seemed they were prepared to pay any price. As the young Americans arrived it dawned on us not too slowly they were all hooked on drugs, and so was a young Englishman – James Fox. The rest of the English contingent whom we knew seemed to have kept an even keel. There was Bryan Forbes and his wife Nanette Newman; we saw a lot of John Standing; and Margaret Leighton, who had, at last, found happiness with Michael Wilding; and Tom Courtenay, who assured me he was in love with Natalie Wood but not getting very far with his overtures. Johnny and Mary Mills were also there, because, very modestly, Johnny had agreed to play a small part in *King Rat*. Hayley was with them, trying to establish herself as a grown-up actress after an overwhelming time as a child star. Jimmy took me on the set and I was glad to hear from all sides nice things said about James, his professionalism and his good manners, the latter being rather rare, I felt.

I could see he had never looked better. The life he had chosen to lead had not yet made inroads on his appearance or his personality, but we were well aware of what the consequences must be and could do no more to prevent them than we could have prevented any illness which might prove fatal. We left for New York feeling sad and inadequate as parents; the prospect of what might happen to James was deeply shattering to Robin.

Still, in New York even Robin enjoyed Carol Channing in *Hello, Dolly*. We found somewhere to have a drink in the interval and Robin said, 'It's not really my favourite sort of evening, but

I do love a big star and Carol Channing certainly is that, and I know that in the next half she's going to come on stage, walk down that long staircase, and look at her funny little lover, then she's going to sing, "Hello, Harry", and I'm going to cry.' In fact, she walked down the staircase, she ignored her little lover, she came to the footlights and sang 'Hello, Robin, I'm so glad to see you back where you belong.' Belong or not, he would have died for that moment. Over the years, on rare and magic occasions, Robin would sit in his seat quietly after a curtain came down and say to me, 'Well, there you are: a performance like that makes it all worthwhile.'

We returned to England to the usual round of hard work and entertaining: the flat at Eaton Square was now quite a haunt for some of the younger writers of the day. I particularly remember John Osborne and Harold Pinter coming to see Robin, and I should like to be able to tell amusing stories about them. However, these two clever boys were speechless and appeared ill at ease no matter how much one bent over backwards to relieve the situation, and entertain the fantasy that this could become a convivial evening. They would merely stare at me very hard with a look I remember to this day as full of loathing and resentment. They certainly forced my feet to the ground.

*

The die was cast and James was now part of the Hollywood drug scene. Even so, we had not pictured in any way the near-junkie who soon turned up in England with a scarecrow whom he introduced as his girlfriend. Drugs were not enough for her; she had added anorexia nervosa to the problem, or it may have been part of it. In his honest book *Comeback*, James refers to her as Amanda, and I shall do the same.

Among the many tasks awaiting Robin now at his office desk was the finalizing of a contract for James to star with Vanessa Redgrave: she was playing Isadora Duncan and he was to be her Gordon Craig. This was ready for James's signature on his return, accompanied by Amanda.

This film was a disaster from the beginning. James was as much suited to play Gordon Craig as he would have been to play Tinker Bell in *Peter Pan*. The real bad luck was that he knew this himself, but what wrecked everything was that having nearly completed the picture, he broke his contract and vanished. He had run into that wonderful actor, Trevor Howard, who was off to some film festival in Brazil and linking the trip with some cricket he was going to see; cricket was his great love. James got it firmly into his head that he would go too and go he did. No remonstration or argument could dissuade him from this sudden, apparently impulsive decision.

Until this time it had always been impossible for Robin to let anyone see him lose his cool, no matter what the situation. But this time his anger knew no bounds, and although he was unwell with some infection and had a high temperature, he set off for Brazil in pursuit of his errant son. He was only away for about a week and returned having failed completely to persuade James to come home, to fulfil his contract and face his obligations. The boy was adamant: not only would he not come home, he intended to journey up the Amazon.

Before James went away he had bought, near Wandsworth Common, a Victorian house with an old-fashioned garden which led into Spencer Park. While he was away I didn't see anything of Amanda: she must have returned temporarily to America. But she was certainly around when, to our surprise, James returned into our midst, fit and well, having himself made a short but exciting and impressive film about his Amazon adventure. He and Amanda moved into the Wandsworth house and now they went downhill, not in a slow descent but in a landslide. It seemed they had made a contract to destroy each other, mentally and physically. In fact, at that moment when his very existence was in such an appalling mess, James tried to explain to both of us that he knew what he was doing was wrong and insane on all counts, but that he couldn't live without his junkie any more than he could live with her. It was at that moment of crisis that he found the courage to have Amanda flown back to California, with a medically trained person to look after her.

Immediately after her departure James set about the task of pulling himself back from destruction. The house on Wandsworth Common became a symbol of his achievement. Slowly and methodically, he turned it from a dirty, disused ruin into a house suitable for a family. He made it comfortable. He bought a number of pieces from Cliveden when the Astors were selling their furniture. He talked to me about what he should do with the garden; we even enjoyed some days together buying old-fashioned roses. He grew interested in Spencer Park and helped with money and with time to restore this rather unique bit of London. In appearance he altered too: the King's Road, Chelsea gear he had taken to wearing was discarded and once again he wore fairly conventional clothes. He was still thin and pale and had the look of a man recovering from a terrible illness, as indeed anyone struggling to kick an addiction to hard drugs is, but his health started to improve.

My impression is that he achieved his cure on his own and was intensely lonely; perhaps it had been loneliness that had unduly influenced the course his life had taken up to then. When we were together he was now polite and very quiet but he had lost all power to communicate with us except on a very superficial, social level. We were like strangers who had just met but who had one or two interests in common. He let us into parts of his life that he didn't mind us knowing. I thought this perfectly normal but was surprised when he invited his father and me to a party at a pub, the Thomas à Becket, in the Old Kent Road. He told us that Henry Cooper, the boxer, had a gym in the upper part of the building where he trained young boxers, and that he himself visited this gym a lot: it was here that he received much help in getting fit. When we arrived, the huge bar was packed with the toughest men I have ever met in my life. There were groups of very pretty girls but all the evening they stayed close together. When I asked one of the men why this was, he told me quite curtly that if they talked with any man other than their own boyfriend, they'd get their faces slapped so hard they might never recover. I enjoyed the whole evening hugely but I do remember Robin kicking me very hard on the shin, and saying to me quietly, 'Don't be *too* naive.'

By the time James had made the film *Performance*, he actually was finished with the drug scene. He not only acted in the film, he had money in it and an interest in the writing and direction and production – he gave it some of the flavour and authenticity of background he had learned at the Thomas à Becket. The crowd there were on the criminal fringe, but good husbands and fathers – and loyal friends: James kept in touch with some of them, and later they came to his wedding and back to Cuckfield with their wives.

*

There are so many sides to this second son, most of which surprise me, but none so much as the next one he revealed: James took it into his head that he wanted to play in the straight theatre. So he decided he would play Henry V at Bath. It gave him his first experience of real failure. Unabashed because, after all, he was still a big film name, James announced next that he would play in comedy, and opened in Blackpool on a Boxing Day in *Doctor in the House* in the part his great friend and mentor, Dirk Bogarde, had played on film. He failed here as well.

Failure and profound loneliness made James a target for

almost anyone who approached him with a suggestion he felt
might at that moment assuage his despair. So when a stranger
from Manchester called Marks came up to him in the Blackpool hotel and asked if he would like to become a Born
Again Christian, James was a sitting duck. Before we knew
where we were, he informed us that he had become an Evangelist and had joined an American religious group called the
Navigators.

Robin and I were dumbfounded and intensely unhappy.
Robin, who was already a sick man, though we did not know it
as yet, seemed further ravaged by this new waywardness of James.
I used laughter as my weapon against what I didn't understand.
I think I was very cruel. Certainly I was not a help to my son,
and we were at war; but still we met and talked, or, to be more
accurate, argued.

Alec Guinness, a Roman Catholic, had a moderating influence
on me, however, a little later. He expressed the view that James
should be treated with very special delicacy and that I, as an
agnostic, might gain some insight into James's state of religious
enthusiasm by reading William James's *Varieties of Religious
Experience*; to gain 'a firmer foothold on very slippery ground',
Alec said.

There is only one absolute lesson that I have learned from
this, and that is that I loved James as much as I am capable of
loving anyone. But in no way did I understand how this actual
addiction came about: my ignorance on the subject of drugs was
abysmal, my unhappiness like a bottomless pit, which was no
help to anyone. So I simply made a vow that physically and
metaphorically I would never shut a door in his face. I kept to
this, and as a result many of the most violent scenes of the crisis
took place in and around our home. I don't think I did widen
my understanding but I gained a reward: James is very good
friends with me now, and he and his family are continually
walking through the open door. His recovery, and the happiness
he finally enjoys, seem entirely due to Mary, the girl he met with
the Navigators. They married and have five children, and I laugh

with and take pleasure in them all. Why do parents waste time crying? His career is flourishing again, too, most recently in *A Passage to India*.

*

After Leslie Grade's incapacitating stroke, he and Robin could of course no longer continue together in partnership. Shortly before this, however, Lol Evans, Robin's former colleague at MCA, had found himself in a very difficult position there. Some deal they had made – I believe with Warner Brothers – made it impossible for MCA to act as an agency as well, and so Lol was about to be at a loose end. Very soon Robin and Lol formed a company of their own, the International Famous Agency, and again I was furnishing offices, this time in Park House between Grosvenor Square and Oxford Street. These offices really became the international headquarters for pretty well all of the big stars in Britain and America, and many from the Continent as well.

Lol and Robin had a very deep friendship, much of it based on the jokes they shared together. A famous anglophile American film star, getting socially a bit big for his boots, succeeded in inviting to dinner some well-known members of the Royal Family. A few theatrical friends were invited to come in after dinner to amuse the guests. 'What a bloody cheek,' said Robin, who, along with Lol, was one of those invited. 'Who does he think we are – a lot of bloody mummers?' Both men were good mimics, so an hour before dinner was to be served – when the host's hysterical anticipation of the honour about to be conferred on his house was at its highest, and when boiling saucepans and spitting ovens were also at their peak – the telephone rang. The host was summoned at once by the butler (probably hired for the night) to be informed by an authoritative voice that he was from the Gas Board, that there was a dangerous leak, that the road immediately outside the house was to be dug up straight away and that to avoid the danger of explosion, all electricity must be cut off for several hours at least: 'It's candles tonight, sir, I'm afraid.' The dinner could not be cancelled, and the courageous anglophile kept his honour while these naughty, grown-up schoolboys enjoyed their joke.

On many occasions Robin and Lol went to America together and had a marvellous time, working and playing and making very big deals. On one of these high-powered trips they sold their business and themselves to an American called Marvin Josephson, who still owns the powerful firm of which Lol Evans is chairman in London. This involved a great deal of money for us.

When he had time Robin constantly worried himself about the two older boys. The youngest one went through the usual adolescent problems while he was still at Harrow, though this didn't really disturb his father, who looked upon them as natural and inevitable. But Robin did get to look very thin and very tired and he developed a slight but ceaseless cough, and complained a little of a nagging pain between his shoulder blades. None of this, however, prepared me. I sat at my looking-glass one Friday evening, making up my face because he was due home at any moment and we were dining with young friends. I heard the car, I heard the door slam – the sounds of a thousand Fridays. He stood in the doorway of our room. I hardly looked up. 'Hello, darling, how are you?'

'Well, not very happy, I'd say. I went for a checkup at the Institute of Directors and they found I have a shadow on my lung.'

PART FOUR

12

The Merchant of Hope

'A shadow on my lung.' A bomb had dropped. Total silence
followed, broken by a silly remark from me when I thought I
could control all signs of emotion. 'At least it's not cancer, you're
too fat for that.' How could I have said it? He had never been
fat in his life and certainly wasn't now. I glanced at him briefly.
He was looking a bit tired, which was quite usual on Friday
evening after a hard week; otherwise he seemed his usual self.
Silence took over again. He went to change for dinner, saying
'We mustn't be late.'

'Wouldn't you like to put them off?'

'And what good would that do?'

So we went to dinner with the Kenneth Kleinworts and Kenneth's first wife, Davina, and a group of friends much younger
than ourselves. I watched Robin. To an outsider his behaviour
would have appeared perfectly normal; but we had driven to the
dinner party in silence and we drove home in silence.

He didn't stay downstairs for his usual last whisky and soda
but went to our bedroom immediately. I followed and noticed
that he just lay still on the bed, and didn't speak or pick up his
book, which was his habit. It was when I went to say good night
that I saw his face was wet with tears, something I had never
seen before in all our years together, except once when he
answered the telephone late one night and was told that Neville
Blond was dying.

There was absolutely nothing I could do or say except take his hand in mine. We stayed like that for hours, because it wasn't until the morning that we could set about trying to do something to remove the shadow from his lung and from our life.

I am never sure whether Robin's physical health was ever totally restored after his war-time lung injury. I remember on his return he had teasingly comforted James, explaining the large scar behind his right shoulder blade as the mark left by a giant spider. It was a great anguish to feel that worry over James had played a part in wearing Robin down. I mean no blame to James in saying that: the young haven't the faintest knowledge of the power they wield, all unconsciously, over other people. James at that time was heedless of his own life and unaware of the effect this had, especially, on his father.

The first person who, at my request, arrived very early to see us was Cocky Farr, before all the London contacts to be made were even awake. He questioned Robin closely about what he had actually been told. In fact the shadow had been diagnosed very definitely as cancer, and Robin already had an appointment early the following morning to see an eminent consultant to find out what action should be taken. Cocky had some coffee with us and when Robin went to have his bath and dress suggested I strolled with him in the garden. It was a May morning of great beauty and Cocky told me the truth. He knew me very well: he had never lied to me in the past and he didn't pull his punches now. He told me that in his opinion, just from what he had heard, Robin would be dead in nine months. He warned me that in our world we were important and that the wool would be pulled over our eyes, many lies told to us to soften the blow, to foster the idea that perhaps miracles could happen. Everything happened exactly as he said, and now I wish I had left Robin's fate in Cocky's hands. He would have got first-class help from chest specialists attached to his own hospital; they wouldn't have saved his life but the hopeless, heartless passage we embarked on would have been avoided.

It seemed that a great committee formed round Robin and

myself. Control of his life began to slip out of our hands but I know now that there are times when acceptance is the only attitude that can be adopted. Michael Sieff was Commander-in-Chief, my son Edward a Brigade Major, and Rosalind Chatto in charge of signals. The staff was enormous and included nearly all the theatrical names in London, every one inspired by a very real desire to help a friend in extreme need.

I went with Robin to London. The eminent doctor asked to see me after he had talked with Robin and told me he thought Robin should have an enormous operation – Cocky had already warned me against this – and he was trying to decide whether to advise Robin to go to the Brompton Hospital or to a local hospital in Sussex. Finally he thought he would plump for the latter. When I asked his reasons for this, he replied that he thought the Sussex hospital was a good one and that it would be much more pleasant for me, visiting Robin, to be in the country, and not too far from home, which he understood was *charming*, in the beautiful May weather. This reasoning astonished me. I had never been in the Brompton Hospital in my life but I was aware of its reputation as one of the finest chest hospitals in the world. Sir Kenneth was insistent, however. I am still covered with bruises – I will be all my life – where I kick myself for being so weak as to have followed this spurious advice, but follow it I did. I was more capable of making a decision than Robin, and my misjudgment added to his suffering.

Edward Sieff, Michael's uncle, had been ill with TB in this country hospital. He had been wonderfully well treated and in gratitude had given the place a great deal of financial help. It was he who arranged for Robin to be admitted and given the best accommodation. I have stressed, I hope, what a courageous man Robin was, but when, on admittance, he was told they would immediately perform a bronchoscopy, he asked most firmly that this should be done under anaesthetic. His request was ignored and the bronchoscopy was performed with no anaesthesia. When I saw him soon after I was appalled by its effect and, what was worse, they hadn't been able to find whatever they were looking for in his lung. In any case the operation was announced for the next day.

The hospital was an hour away and by the time I arrived next morning the operation had already been performed. I learned only then that the best qualified surgeon was on holiday. The man who had done it was vastly experienced but about eighty, and had been called in as a locum while the specialist was away. I only saw him once – this was moments after I arrived – and it took him only two minutes to tell me that Robin's entire chest was riddled with cancer.

Robin didn't die as a result of this operation but to a lay person like myself it seemed that he must have been a very strong man to survive the mess that was made of him. But this expensive excavation, totally unnecessary in my opinion now, caused the disease to spread quickly and accelerated debilitation, so that even while he was trying to recover from the effect of the operation, he started to fall down continually.

Cocky kept me informed as to the course the illness was taking. He told me that Robin now had tumours on his brain – they were not the result of radiotherapy, though I would be told this was so. He was absolutely right – there is not one lie in the book I wasn't told by the smart, expensive doctors of the day. Had we not been so well off and – in a way – important, Robin would have died, as so many do, from lung cancer; but the illness might have been accepted more, and his death would have been a little calmer and easier. As it was, no stone was left unturned and with the best of intentions. Treatments and discussions and consultations drifted on until the autumn, with Robin's condition always deteriorating.

Before being taken ill Robin had seen some rehearsals of *Home* by David Storey, with John Gielgud and Ralph Richardson. He was too ill to go to the opening night but when he was trying to pick up the threads after that, we had a box to see a performance and he was very moved. We managed to get him backstage, frail as he was, to see John Gielgud, who was changed and ready and waiting for him with Robin's favourite brand of whisky on the table. John and he talked together for a long time. This sensitive man's kindness meant a great deal to Robin. It was when Robin was on the telephone to New York after this, negotiating the American deal for *Home* which would take Gielgud and Richardson to Broadway, that he had his first fit, and we knew for certain that the cancer had spread to his brain.

When Robin knew he was dying he had only one wish: to visit Dirk Bogarde at his house in the South of France. Of all Robin's clients, Dirk was now the closest. I had first met him when James was engaged to play the boy in *The Servant*. He then had a house at Hascombe, near Guildford, with a lovely garden, something one inevitably associates with Dirk. Several times Robin and I had also stayed at a house he rented just outside Rome. At one time when we were there I had had jaundice, and Dirk did all the cooking himself, and took so much trouble to see that I ate correctly and make me rest that I owe my complete recovery to him. Dirk is a fine gardener and a good cook, can scrub a kitchen floor even better than I can and – above all – he thinks nothing of doing it if there is no one else. He also draws most beautifully. And all the world now knows how good a writer he is.

Dirk is the perfect friend, but the thing that used to interest me was his professionalism: he understood everything about film-making and is the most reliable and dependable actor I have ever watched work. And still he cares so passionately about getting it right that he can be a nervous wreck at the end of a picture. He really cares.

*

We were advised that Robin should not fly and so we went by train. He was far too ill to undertake this, and the journey wasn't like pre-war days as we spoilt Foxes remembered it. It was a nightmare of discomfort and we were very, very late arriving. Dirk was in the most nervous state I had ever seen him in because he'd just finished *Death in Venice*; the sight of his friend Robin must have given him an appalling shock.

Staying at the house were Daphne and Xan Fielding: Daphne had been married to Lord Bath and had given up Longleat and all that life for Xan. Robin promptly had a fit on arrival. This was awful for Dirk, but Xan came to my rescue and when Robin came round the first thing he asked was, 'Who is the little killer at the end of the bed?' The description certainly fitted Xan, who had worked with the underground in Greece during the war. He was a great help and when the French doctor arrived he acted as interpreter – not that there was anything anyone could do. Daphne was so kind and before leaving gave me her supply of valium, which I would not take.

Robin struggled to dress every day and once he said he wanted to look at 'Dependence', the house next to Dirk's that he had hoped to buy. This meant his walking perhaps five hundred yards. This once athletic man managed about fifty and then collapsed. It was such pain for Dirk to see the man he depended on and loved in this hopeless state. I was grateful for all the kindness but I had one thought: how to get Robin home. And then a forest fire broke out; the surrounding forest and country-side burst into flames with the wind blowing it in our direction. It seems to me now that hell was getting nearer and nearer.

Robin's terrible illness was taking its inevitable course. He could never get away from it and though I was always with him, I thought I would be in better form, and more help, if I had a short break so I went for forty-eight hours to stay with Edward in Norfolk at a cottage he was renting at Clay-next-the-Sea while he was filming *The Go-Between*.

Edward's dear girlfriend during this period, Eileen Atkins, had joined him and because they were so happy together – something I wasn't used to – I spent a good time with them, a lot of it walking by the sea with Eileen in a howling gale. Joe Losey and his girlfriend came for dinner. I just had time to be reminded of Joe's two sides: to dine with him was to be with a dull, groaning, humourless American but on the set, where I saw him working briefly the next day, he was a creative, authoritative, brilliant and positive director.

I was grateful to Eileen and Edward for this break. I had no armour against illness; it terrified and horrified me. Even when my children had been ill fear made me useless and I would try to run away. I was about to learn that, finally, you cannot.

Robin now summoned the last energy he had left and told me he wasn't going to give in, that he wanted to try anything he could on God's earth to prove the pundits of the medical profession wrong, and would I get hold of Cocky? I did as he asked and Cocky came to London. I remember him sitting facing Robin at the end of his bed, and Robin had a list for Cocky. He wanted to know in detail exactly what would happen to him. Cocky answered all the questions truthfully, each one more gruesome than the last. Finally, Robin asked, 'Shall I go insane?' Cocky said yes. Robin turned to me and said quite calmly, 'Well, then, we can't have that, can we? I loathe the Germans, but somehow we'll have to get to the Clinic in Munich and see what that bloody Issels can do.'

There had recently been a programme on BBC television about the Issels Clinic. Issels was a Bavarian with star quality who put over brilliantly his conviction that he could cure those terminally ill with cancer. I didn't know at the time that two eminent British doctors, Professor Sir David Smithers and Professor Hamilton, objected to the film's favourable attitude towards Issels' technique. The personality of the man had a magnetic effect on those suffering, together with their distraught dependants. The programme had made an enormous impact on the British public and people with cancer were rushing to Issels' clinic. It was already practically impossible to get in. But again, because of influence and money – and after long conversations on the telephone – Issels agreed for Robin to go there.

So we flew to Munich. Michael Sieff, as well as organizing everything, accompanied James, Robin and me. James was still living in Wandsworth, and was now an Evangelist. He and I were tied in knots of misery although we didn't say anything and, once again, I remember Robin with admiration because although his sight was beginning to go, during the flight he calmly read *The Times* from cover to cover. He appeared able to detach himself from the purpose of this odd journey.

Munich Airport before the Olympics was a very hole-in-the-corner dump but we were through Customs very quickly and an enormous Mercedes with chauffeur was waiting to drive us to Rottachegern, part of the village of Tergensee in Bavaria at the foot of the mountains, where the Clinic was situated. Shortly before we got there I noticed to the right a signpost to Dachau, enough to make anyone's heart drop. In outward appearance the Clinic was fairly typical of a large Bavarian chalet. There were a lot of smaller houses in the grounds, each one of them housing patients of all nationalities, all ages, and all dying of cancer.

Dr Issels knew very well that Robin was a tycoon with a strong influence in the world of television, so he was to be housed in the main building. Although his room seemed no bigger than a large cupboard it did have its own balcony and a beautiful outlook to snow-covered mountains, and this was a luxury – the only one. Despite Robin's importance he was kept waiting a long time. Given the unfavourable publicity Issels received later, it is hard not to believe that the waiting was part of the treatment: Issels' own manner did everything to create an aura of self-importance, for he was as much a guru as a conventional physician.

Our party sat miserably in the downstairs hall which had a staircase leading up to the patients' rooms. No one came near us for a long time until, finally, Michael Sieff set about demanding some show of awareness that we had arrived. He did this through the office, which led from the hall. A pleasant, rather good-looking, animated woman arrived. She introduced herself in good English as Eleanor Melle and said she was the person in overall charge of administration of the buildings and the patients, but that she could not show Robin to his room until Dr Issels had seen him. Naturally we expected that he would be summoned to a consulting room. That was a mistaken notion. Suddenly the boss himself swept into the hall, followed by a subservient entourage, all carrying pads of paper on which they wrote down his barked instructions. These instructions were in German, so as far as we were concerned they could have been 'Three Blind Mice', but it was all part of the showmanship.

Showman Issels was handsome, with very thick, beautifully barbered snow-white hair; very blue, very severe, pale blue eyes; a high-coloured, rather swarthy complexion. He always wore an immaculate, long white coat, white silk shirt, white silk tie, white trousers, white suede shoes. Without hesitation he walked straight to Robin: he knew none of the rest of us was ill. He said really very little to Robin except which room he was to occupy and that he would be visiting him first thing in the morning. He then turned on his heel and swept away, entourage in pursuit.

I was slightly impressed – I almost giggled – but any good feeling I had passed in a flash when Robin said, 'He stinks of drink, stale white wine.' ·

*

Robin was at the Issels Clinic for nine and a half weeks. I was one of the very, very lucky dependants because I lived in a luxurious hotel, the Bachmeier, in great comfort. The other dependants of patients I got to know closely all seemed to be staying at a spotlessly clean gasthaus, the only one that would take people connected with the infamous – in their eyes – Issels Clinic. I had a beautiful room at the Bachmeier, and the restaurant was as fine as any in the world, but even as I signed the reception book on the first evening I sensed that sooner than hear about the Clinic the hotel people would rather not know of its existence: there would never be any communication on that score. I was a visitor and their attitude to me for all those weeks was one of impersonal politeness.

No time was lost before Robin's ordeal began. Issels swept into his room the next day, still followed by his acolytes and sat on Robin's bed, charm personified. He put up the palm of his hand facing Robin and asked his new patient to put his own hand against it. He was no longer pretending he couldn't speak English. He could – not fluently, but adequately. He said, 'Put your hand against mine. Now press as hard as you can. Push my hand away and I will resist you.' Already Robin was so weak he couldn't begin to push this hand out of the way. Issels, very hearty and all smiles, said, 'But you will, you will see, you will grow strong again and push me away from you and will be well again and walk out of my Clinic. But you must do everything I tell you. I must never be disobeyed, and together we will have hope and we will succeed and you will be better.'

In this uplifting and edifying speech the word that kept us in the Clinic for nine weeks, obeying the worthless orders of this man to the letter, was 'hope'. I had no hope in my heart, but for five weeks Robin had, and for this I am grateful.

We were given our first instructions. Robin was to have an injection which would immediately cause his temperature to become very, very high. The injection was the nurse's job but when Robin reached a state of raging fever, I was to nurse him. There was a staff at the Clinic, but from the point of view of numbers, it was inadequate. The dependants of the patients had to take on much of the responsibility for looking after them: this was an integral part of the 'cure'. Yet it was a matter of life and death, and I confess to being the most unsuitable candidate in the world for this appalling role – and appalling it became.

The forcing of the temperature to rise was the least dreadful item on the programme. I learned from doctors of different nationalities who visited the Clinic while we were there that this and other drugs administered to Robin were, in fact, used internationally but that in Robin's case even a student would have known they were totally useless. Issels was vastly experienced but nevertheless this was his method, a drastic approach which he claimed produced remarkable remissions. How rare these were we didn't know at the time. (Twenty-two out of eight thousand cases were thus described later in a book Issels wrote.)

Robin did everything exactly as he was told. He never once

complained. He grew weaker and more nauseated every day, and Issels would command him and other dying patients to get dressed and walk hard in the snow. It was agony to see, because Robin was holding on to hope, so he was as obedient as a defenceless child.

The whole scene became more and more macabre and cruel. Edward was busy in Norfolk in *The Go-Between* but the moment it was finished, he threw in his hand, he gave up everything, his career and his girl, to come to Germany and help nurse Robin. James sat and read his Bible and I did the best I could; James had tried to share his new-found religion with me. It was a bad moment for us all and I rejected his offer. Not meaning to, he distressed his father over this but he was wonderfully kind to children suffering from cancer, and to children who were there because a parent was dying. He bought sledges and toboggans and played for hours, for days, with them. Michael Sieff came every weekend and Robert Morley would catch the Sunday morning plane and stay as long as he could before getting the flight back in time for his evening performance on Mondays. I was one of the very, very fortunate people among those suffering agonies of unhappiness at this Clinic.

I attended a lot of deaths on this floor for the terminally ill, the first very soon after my arrival. He was an Italian of about thirty-seven, with a very pretty blonde wife who had shown me round as soon as I arrived – as she explained, there was no one else to do so. She had told me she had two children she had left in the care of her mother, that her husband was an industrialist, that now he was dying. She could afford to take him home, and she wished she could but he was now too ill: she had missed her chance.

Before I had been in the Clinic a week, she called me in terrible distress one evening and said her husband was choking. Horrified, I went with her to his room. There was a male and a female nurse with him, giving him all the kindness and care they possibly could. The patient was in agony and, worse than that, he was petrified. I managed to gather that the nurses couldn't sedate him because Issels had left no instructions for sufficient drugs, and Issels' word was total law. I found Eleanor Melle and told her to telephone Issels. I saw at once that she was frightened of him too; she said she could not do it. I told her to get the number, as I didn't know how to, and I would speak to him. She was furious then as well as frightened but I insisted. What a waste of time. I put down the receiver and went back to the room to report failure. Fortunately there was no need to tell them. The man was dead.

There were a number of insufferable experiences like that, and I mention this example because I wouldn't like it thought that I imagined for a moment the experience I had was in any way worse for me or for Robin than for other people who found themselves paying a price for such false hopes as Issels advertised.

On one occasion Michael Sieff brought with him from London a doctor called Emmanuel Herbert, a respected man who had been trained in Vienna and had a huge practice in London. He had come to see if Issels' claim had any elements of truth. He was charming to me and told me immediately he saw no point in Robin remaining here: were Robin his patient, he would arrange for his immediate return to England. But Robin still had hope. He and Edward, in their different roles, behaved like two fanatics, the father refusing to be defeated, the son refusing to believe that the battle for Robin to live could not be won. Between them, they carried out every one of Issels' instructions.

Herr Doktor never missed a trick. He saw very quickly that I had no faith in him whatsoever but naturally he had no wish to alienate influential people, knowing that the man with us, Michael Sieff, would help him financially with his Clinic if, by some extraordinary fluke, Robin did not die. I believe he also had a fanatical belief that he was so brilliant he might beat cancer. However it was, Issels set out to try to be polite to Mrs Fox. He said he was giving a dinner party for me and Michael, who accepted immediately and told me I was a fool if I made an enemy of the man. There could be no doubt he was right about that, and so to dinner we went.

Issels lived in a magnificent house and we had a most luxurious evening, ending up with everyone in a typical German *Bierkeller*, drinking a great deal – it reminded one of a film in which a very famous star of olden days, called Conrad Veidt, would have played the Doctor. The whole set-up was more theatrical than anything I can remember in a long life in show business. The first surprise was that off-duty Issels chain-smoked – yet he would erupt in fury if a distraught dependant of a patient even lit a cigarette in the big garden of the Clinic, yelling things like: 'Murderer! Are you so stupid not to realize that what you are doing is the cause of cancer?'

*

The Clinic routine we found most agonizing was the dictum that an adult's or child's teeth and tonsils must be taken out without an anaesthetic of any sort. The theory behind this, as described by a British Inquiry set up after the death of Lillian Board, who was a patient of Issels at the same time as Robin, was that the whole body must be treated. The extractions took place daily in a room immediately below Robin's; the screams of pain and of fear were horrible. Fortunately, Robin spent more and more hours in a semi-conscious state, caring less and less what happened. Perhaps I now need a psychiatrist to tell me what I minded most.

Issels then instructed that Robin was to be given a drug called endoxana: this would make him sick very frequently, the sickness lasting possibly three days, possibly three weeks. What also had to be faced was that every hair on his head would fall out. Robin had wonderful hair; it grew beautifully, it was thick and dark and I had always enjoyed the fact that he was a vain man who thought his own appearance, indeed everybody's, was of vital importance. Issels had watched me when he told us about it. We never spoke, but he knew us very well. He knew how much I cared, the pain of it and what the loss of Robin's hair symbolized to me. They told us that the nurse would give Robin this drug very early in the morning. Robin was quiet and semi-conscious, but the nurse didn't arrive early and I sat with him all day, waiting for someone to walk in to administer this dose. Finally she came at about six o'clock that evening. I hope I am not morbid but I sat and looked at Robin all day, hating the destruction of this rather splendid man.

Everything then happened exactly as Issels had taken care to explain it would – only it was worse than my wildest dreams. Robin never stopped being sick and after ten days I telephoned to Cocky Farr in England and begged him to come out: I would, of course, pay everything and make all the arrangements. Cocky did as I asked and got to us as quickly as he could. He was appalled at Robin's condition. He knew all about the drug and said that it was used a great deal in England for certain forms of cancer, but that only an extremely unconventional practitioner would have administered it to Robin because he must have known that it couldn't now be effective; it was more likely to cause unspeakable discomfort and suffering. Cocky also told me he could tell by Robin's appearance that it was, if anything, hastening his end because his kidneys were collapsing under the strain.

In all this time of unhappiness there was – as indeed there always is, if you can accept it – help and mercy at hand. At one point I had to return to England for a few days because our flat in Eaton Square had been ransacked by burglars – there had been a small piece in the press saying that impresario Robin Fox had gone to Germany to seek a cure for terminal cancer, so the burglars knew the flat would be empty. They had taken everything most precious to us, including an exquisite, quite small collection of Fabergé pieces Robin's father had left him, and which he really treasured; several boxes, some studs and cuff links, a number of tiepins and above all a watch, its face surrounded by sapphires, that he always wore at night. There was nothing I could do. I arrived too late. Although the police were wonderful, they told me this type of article would vanish only too quickly.

But on the aeroplane back to Munich I was befriended by a

delightful German woman, Gi Pretty, who was married to an Englishman. She was going to visit her sister, the Baronin Helga von Frankenborg, wife of one of the heads of Siemens in Munich. She comforted me on the journey. I think, without dramatizing things, it must have been quite easy to see that I was a woman at breaking point. Gi told me that no one in Munich in the world of orthodox medicine accepted that Issels was anything but a mountebank and an adventurer, and that his very name was loathed. I couldn't say this came exactly as a surprise: I had sensed that attitude although I spoke not one word of German. Of course we didn't know this, but later we found out that in 1960 Issels had been arrested on charges of fraud and manslaughter (although after his conviction, judgment was reversed on appeal).

When we arrived at the airport, Gi's sister was there to meet her. They were influential people so we were able to go to a small office in the airport where Gi told Helga of my plight, adding that we must all hurry as there were no staff to nurse Robin at night and, as I had told her, it was my turn. So Helga said she would be over in the morning to see what she could do for me, and I set off on the two-hour drive.

I made Robin as comfortable as I could for the night and told Edward to go and get some dinner. Imagine my surprise when suddenly in the doorway stood Helga von Frankenborg. She was very firm and told me I was to go back to my hotel and go to bed, that she had been trained as a nurse in the war and that she would stay with Robin and make arrangements to have proper night nurses sent out from Munich as soon as possible. She also thought I ought to insist that a day nurse be sent out from England. She told me later she felt Robin should not have been left for one moment without full-time nursing. I did everything she said and an Irish nurse flew out to us within twenty-four hours; she was an enormous help.

*

I saw Helga and Gi Pretty almost every day. They had a chalet in the mountains nearby and came out to be with me. They offered to make the chalet absolutely free for me or my sons or for any of our friends, but by this time I was too distraught – Robin was so ill – to accept their kind offer. Helga and her husband talked with the doctors in Munich and finally took it upon themselves to arrange for an orthodox neurologist to visit Robin and make the decision they knew I was incapable of, namely for him to be flown back to England as quickly as possible so that he could die in the comfort of his own home, away from what had become hell for the dying – and for the living.

I remember waiting for this man and growing very anxious when he was late. In fact, he had arrived at the Clinic at the arranged time but had been told that Herr Fox had already been flown back to England. By pure chance I went out into the corridor where I heard a very angry man talking in German about Herr Fox. I realized he was the neurologist, and took him into Robin's room where Cocky Farr was sitting with him. He examined the patient briskly, kindly and thoroughly, then said he would like to speak to me outside.

'Your husband is dying. There is absolutely no hope. He is blind. I asked him to look at the picture above his bed – of trees and a lot of men in a street – and he told me that it was of the sea and boats. He is a very brave man and very tired and I don't think he has more than a few days to be in this world. Go as soon as you can make arrangements.' He bowed, kissed my hand and vanished. But he left me with courage.

Issels came that night and announced with his usual ingratiating and confident authority that he was going to step up the strength of this drug he was giving Robin. At that moment I was no longer the feeble idiot I believe I have been all my life. I remember standing up and saying, 'Oh no you're not. We're leaving. I'm going now to make the arrangements.' Issels' rage at being crossed was as violent as anything I have ever encountered. I told him to get out of the room and stay out of our lives now and for ever. We were leaving.

With the help of the von Frankenborgs I got reservations for England. There were rather a lot of us. Apart from family – Edward didn't agree with my decision – there were Ros Chatto, Robin's friend and former manager whom I had asked to come to the Clinic because I heard him say her name, Cocky, the Irish nurse and myself. But we managed to get reservations on one of the few aeroplanes going to England the next day, New Year's Eve 1970.

I had been befriended by taxi drivers and their families during my stay, so I went into town and looked them up because I knew they could get an ambulance for me locally – it was snowing so hard I thought it might be difficult to make the journey from Munich and back again in the morning. They did arrange this, plus a car to take some of us. But Issels had one last defiant throw. Somehow he found out what I had done. When morning came, he had cancelled the ambulance. My taxi-driver friends kept wonderfully cool and somehow got a second car. Issels had given instructions that Robin was to receive no help in leaving, so these good men helped carry him down the stairs and out into the thick snow, and somehow we got this big man sort of folded up into one of the taxis. The nurse and Cocky sat beside the driver, the rest of us went in the second car, and somehow we managed to reach Munich airport. There was now one final question – there was a strike in England and it wasn't certain whether we would take off at all. God knows how we got away but we did, and by nightfall, with every arrangement smoothly made by the Sieffs for Robin's journey in England, we were home.

A last, small miracle occurred when the ambulance came into the courtyard at our house at Cuckfield. Robin had what seemed a momentary resurgence of life. He told Cocky he wanted to walk into the house. I had arrived before he had and was standing by the door, and was astounded to see him try to push away people who wanted to help. He walked very slowly and carefully towards me. He was smiling and he said, 'I'm home, and tomorrow I shall see my beautiful garden.' I threw back my head and laughed as I hadn't done for weeks. Robin had not been faintly interested in the garden except to grumble and say that it wasn't quite right. It was a good exit line for him, really, because he was then helped to his own bed which he never left again.

No love and comfort was spared. All his family walked in and out in a perfectly normal way. Cocky's doctoring of him was all one could have wished and Robin's favourite clients who were his dearest friends filled the house. He was hardly ever conscious but they took turns to sit with him and hold his hand. Paul Scofield would do this for hours on end. He once said to me, 'He was always such a good-looking friend and now he's dying he's really beautiful.' Lindsay Anderson also came a great deal and Godfrey Winn came most evenings; he would make me change my dress and make up my face. I can hear him saying, 'Oh pull yourself together, Angie,' and then he would take me out to dinner at the local restaurant. The house was full of friends and life and laughter.

The only person who behaved foolishly, even cruelly, towards me was Joe Losey, who made a hysterical scene and beat his fists against the wall, screaming at me that I was a murderer and that if it had not been for me and my inability to be disciplined enough to stay in Germany, Robin would have been cured: I had killed him. If Joe had meant to upset me he couldn't have been more successful in his efforts. I was very vulnerable on that point – and still am – saying to myself, 'Oh God, did I do the right thing? Or was I lacking in guts because I couldn't take it?' I admit that I couldn't take it but was later relieved, as much as it was possible to be relieved in such circumstances, to hear that largely as the result of a report on Issels' methods by five British cancer specialists after Lillian Board's death, the Clinic closed in 1973. 'Patients do not need to be worried about not being able to go to Dr Issels,' said Professor Sir David Smithers, with masterly understatement. Issels gave his reasons for the closure as 'external influences and sabotage inside the Clinic. The conspiracy has become too big.'

Epilogue

Robin died on 20th January 1971.

Michael Sieff again assumed command and even then I couldn't help smiling that, being Jewish and such a good manager, he insisted that the funeral take place quickly and even got the Protestant vicar to bury his friend on a Saturday. It seemed that all the big names who worked in the English entertainment business were there, and so were all the boys and girls from the Royal Court Theatre, making a very King's Road contingent. They sang, at my choice:

> O God, our help in ages past,
> Our hope in years to come

in Holy Trinity Church, Cuckfield: and by a wonderful coincidence – it's possible Robin arranged it – the crucifix that went ahead of his coffin was carried by a little black girl who sang in the choir. Flowers carpeted all the churchyard and even made a path up towards the village street.

Cocky Farr, a great observer, told us that Robert Morley stood alone in the wind and the rain that January day after all the friends and stars had moved away. Utterly alone, a tragic figure, for once not acting a part, Cocky heard him say, with his head bowed very low, 'So this is really the end.' Then he turned and walked back to our house where the Wake was taking place and became the witty life and soul of a memorable funeral party.

I am not at all ashamed to say that the Wake at Ockenden Cottage was fabulous, the food and drink abundant, the warmth and kindness and love something Robin never knew he had earned. I stood, feeling he was beside me, and talking with our friends, feeling in addition suddenly so grateful for all that life had given us. I was aware that it was a very big theatrical occasion. I also knew that soon they would all be gone and, sure enough, that moment came. Much kissing and hugging, many promises about the future and the wonderful things it was going to hold. And then I walked back into our big sitting room, knowing that it would be empty – and I was wrong. Relaxing in an armchair by the fire was Laurence Olivier and, in the other chair, his wife Joan.

The three Fox boys had followed me into the room. Of course we were all thinking, 'Well, what the hell do we do now?' Larry knew all this. He had known before we did and he had made his plan. He is a very great actor but at that moment he was a very, very great friend, the best anyone could ever have. What he had arranged was quite simple.

'You can't be here alone, you lot. You're following us in your car to our house in Brighton, and we're all going to have a lovely nursery tea with the children and I'm going out to buy the buns.'

He got up.

'Go now, get ready, follow us. If you're not there in half an hour, I shall be on the telephone. I shall not take no for an answer and I don't want you to make me cross.'

He put his arms round me and hugged me and they went.

We were slow in setting out and he *did* have to telephone and he *was* cross, so we did exactly as he said. It was the most terrible winter's day, with penetrating rain and a tremendous gale and very cold. Arriving at his house in Royal Crescent, Brighton, as we got out of the car we saw him advancing towards us. He appeared to be wearing a cape and a sort of Sherlock Holmes hat, and he was battling against the wind and rain and carrying a lot of packages. He really had been out buying cakes and biscuits for the nursery tea.

I sat next to him at this feast and it was a lovely party. He talked to me a bit but he started there and then with an awareness of the boys' grief, youth and need. He told wonderful stories about the theatre and made them exert themselves in recollections and arguments. He had observed us clearly and been generously aware that what we needed was a change of thought as well as of scene. It was quite late at night when we finally left. When he saw us off we were too tired even to be sad, yet in fact he had made our spirits high, and hopes for the future of our family were on the cards again. Let me never forget: great actor, great friend.

*

In the days when Mrs Jones was riding furiously towards The Front to meet Captain Jones, she often thought it would be splendid if he was Dead, because then she could be rather sad and get out of doing all the things she did not want to do and, best of all, she could wear Widow's Weeds. This last thought attracted her very much. In Mrs Jones's day there was a great deal of palaver when husbands died. They were usually Dr Worthington's patients, and so occupied Nanny and Hilda the maid, that it almost seemed to happen in the nursery, so close was the drama. Mrs Jones got very mixed up. She listened to the details spellbound, and with horror at once developed the illness that had proved fatal, nearly always in a state of knowing that she, too, was going to her Maker that day.

All this took a lot out of her, hence the nervous, rather pale-faced child. However, what offset her sense of stress at these stories was the thought of herself wearing Widow's Weeds. This garb was jet-black from top to toe. The skirts were worn long to the ground; on the head was a hat, sometimes a toque though it could have a brim; but over this, whatever the shape, went what Mrs Jones liked best: a very, very heavy veil that fell almost to the waist. Even the gloves were black, the only break anywhere in this ensemble being a tiny, snow-white and if possible lace handkerchief: a black hand would lift the veil and dab the eyes from time to time that were staring sadly from a pale, unpainted face. It seemed that absolutely nothing was asked of the widow but this performance, and she was amply rewarded for it by having everyone do absolutely everything for her. She did not have to speak and, even if the whole episode was a great relief, she never had to let on. All responsibility was taken from her and whatever the effect of the Death of her Partner, it could be anguished over, even recovered from, behind this veil.

When my turn came, this custom – so in tune with the crisis, indeed, so sensible – was no longer the order of the day. I knew I was expected to Dry My Eyes, Pull Myself Together, Put On a Good Face, and above all, Decide What To Do, Make Decisions.

I did all this, announced I was the Merry Widow and made hundreds of decisions, every single one of them, without exception, wrong. In public I laughed a lot, in private I cried so much I used to wonder where the water for these tears was stored. Above all I was possessed by an irrational, inexplicable fear which I spent every ounce of energy trying to hide. It became fear of fear. I recall it as just panic, made more difficult by the fact that I didn't want to worry the boys with this, though I don't suppose they would have minded at all but would have taken it in their stride, as they did everything else. I was asked continually, 'Have you got over your husband's death?' Then and now I always have the same answer, 'Oh yes, but I shall never get over his life.'

Of course self-pity, the worst weakness of all, plays a big part in early widowhood. There's a tendency to hang on to the past. The trouble is, what can one put in its place? There are friends who stretch out their hands to help: one of these was Tyrone Guthrie, the director. I had met him about ten years before when he had directed Robert Morley for us in a very serious play which had failed dismally; but 'Tony', as he was known to his friends, had stayed with me at Cuckfield when they opened at Brighton.

One of the reasons I am sure I really loved him was that we were such poles apart in our values; I being neurotic and over-fastidious about cleanliness and order in domestic life, he having a total disregard for such mundane matters. I had to laugh at myself when Alice, who was unpacking his bags for him, called me and said I had better come and give my advice, as everything was so dirty and in such a mess she didn't know where to start. I took one look and ordinarily would have said, having observed the contents of the suitcase, 'Oh, shut the bloody thing up and stuff it under the bed.' But for Tony my reaction was quite different. With loving care I gathered up all the dirty socks and shirts and pants, staggered with them to my washing machine, and when they were clean, ironed them myself, aired them and placed them in drawers in his room as I had seen my elegant father-in-law's Rose do. That surely was love!

Tony's appearance was unusual: he was enormously tall with rather aquiline features, penetrating eyes and a rather military moustache, an air of breeding; he wore fairly good but very shabby suits and, when I knew him, sand shoes. Once, when he was returning from Brighton to Haywards Heath Station after taking a difficult rehearsal, Cocky Farr had reason to go to the station and volunteered to pick him up. It was bitterly cold and raining so I asked Cocky not to keep him hanging around as I didn't want him to catch a cold. I expected them to be about ten minutes but after half an hour the telephone rang. It was Cocky in a call-box.

'There's nobody like Sir Tyrone here at the station,' he said, 'there's only one huge farmer pacing up and down in a mackintosh.'

'That,' I said, 'is our guest. Get him in the car.'

Tony Guthrie was an intellectual and he had a great love and appreciation of music. The first night he stayed with me we were listening to Mozart when, at eight o'clock, well-trained Alice announced that dinner was ready. When I made a move Tony said sharply, 'Don't fidget, we can't go until the end of the last movement. Don't be insensitive.' The following night he was teaching me something about the music of Bach which I found very difficult to follow; but I had told Alice that I would come to the kitchen and tell her when we were ready to eat, as I did not want to upset Sir Tyrone again. When five past eight came, this genius looked at his watch and said, 'For God's sake, isn't dinner ready? I'm famished, it's past eight o'clock.' Tony Guthrie kept one on one's toes. Another time I remember asking him, 'You will let me know if there's anything else I can do for you?' 'There is something,' he replied. 'Shall we have a little less of the house beautiful?' What good advice for any over-anxious hostess.

Tony's delayed departure was due to the fact that he knew Robert Morley could, if only he would, give a serious and moving performance in the play and, as its director, he hoped his powers of persuasion would prevail. I had a glimpse of Robert Morley taking this advice at a rehearsal, and it was a very moving moment in the theatre. He could have been one of our great actors but he chose this time – and for ever after – just to be our best comedian. Tony had to accept that he had failed and he departed immediately, and then I saw him very seldom; but we wrote long letters to each other frequently.

Tony came to see me very soon after Robin died – the first moment that he could get to England. I remember a sense of overwhelming relief when he walked into the room.

'Why have you come?' I asked.

'Well, because you needed me, of course.'

We talked all night; that is, I talked and he listened. I felt he was tired and should go to bed. He wouldn't agree to that but kept on saying, 'Go on, go on.' About 4.30 a.m. we did go to our rooms and I said, 'Mostly I am so frightened – do you know about fear?' And he replied, 'No' very firmly. For some reason that made me feel stronger. Four days later he was dead, of heart failure that he knew, when he came to help me, would get him if he made any unnecessary effort. Tony's doctor was a friend of mine and told me he had advised him not to come to Cuckfield to comfort me. He had paid not the slightest attention.

*

I had been with Tony Guthrie perhaps a dozen times in my life, but I knew he was the closest and perhaps the most understanding friend I ever had. This doesn't mean he was always polite to me: far from it. He liked Edward very much, too, and one of my last memories was of him sitting in the garden at Ockenden Cottage deep in conversation with Edward; when I went near them Tony said, 'Go away, it's Edward's turn.' A few minutes later he left to go to Gatwick Airport to fly to his home in Ireland.

It is very well known that the most consistent advice Tony ever gave to those he was fond of, who were in any sort of jam, was to 'Rise above it.' When Robin died I felt that if nothing else I was worldly-wise, I knew the score, I knew who my friends were. I was a hundred per cent wrong in this judgment and in many other ways as well. I still had pretty well everything to learn and sometimes the course was very demanding, but finally it has made me laugh; at myself mostly, but also at the unexpected frailty of those I had chosen to think of as so strong and dependable. I learned that it was Robin who had been the strong one.

I have no idea whether it is just imagination or not, but ever since I was widowed I have never had to wait long for some friend, whom I had understood to be dead, to give me a pretty good idea of what I should do. The first person who came vividly into my mind was Gladys Cooper. She reminded me of a time she had described when she thought an aeroplane she was travelling in was going to crash in the Barrier Reef in Australia.

'Oh, Gladys, if that had happened, what would you have done?'

'Walk forward, of course. That is all you can do. Someone or something turns up and then you know what you have to do next.'

At the risk of sounding whimsical, I took Gladys's advice; and every time I was in distress and in a muddle, Tony Guthrie would again join me and laugh and say, as he always did, 'Rise above it.'

I have been joined by a host of friends, now all dead; I talk as often to Godfrey Winn, Archie McIndoe and particularly to Simon Marks as frequently as I ever did. Now that life has got some form and pattern again, I am rather chary of making too many idiotic mistakes, so I can even go and find these friends and ask them what I should do. It means keeping quiet, an unnatural effort for me, but if I do it they never let me down. Relying upon the wisdom and experience of people who have gone on their way can be better than expecting those who are still here with you to be detached and objective – they are still embroiled in working out so many problems of their own, which is quite clearly what we are all still here to do.

In a desire to be useful, I have joined committees. Mostly what I have learned from that was that, as a committee woman, I am, in fact, just the opposite – useless. I sat on the Southeast Branch of the Arts Council for a time. My fellow members were very glad to see the back of me because I never hesitated to tell them I found it a profligate waste of time and energy to give money to young, undisciplined, usually left-wing, grotty semi-professionals who thought that because they were interested in what they referred to as The Arts, they should be financed by the tax-payer. I have no respect for this sickness in modern society and even less respect for the second-rate intellects of my fellow committee members who pandered to them to inflate their own egos.

I did slightly better as Vice-Chairman of the Benevolent Fund for the English National Opera, which I originally joined because of my admiration and respect for Jennie Lee who, I believe, was the best Minister for the Arts we have ever had. It was through this Committee that I have enjoyed a friendship for the last twelve years with George and Patricia Harewood. I have travelled with them several times to the West Indies, and have had good holidays staying with them and their young families at Harewood. George Harewood is one of the people who, without ever talking about it, gave me the confidence to know that I could start enjoying a whole new life. He has done more for opera in England than possibly anyone else. And it was through working at the Coliseum that I made new friends and came across for the first time in my life people connected with music and opera.

In time I sold up Ockenden Cottage but kept a much smaller pair of derelict labourers' cottages which were in the garden, converting one of them into a little house known as Buntings where I now live. There is a pretty, walled garden and just enough room for the boys, their wives and families, to visit.

*

Dirk Bogarde did not come to his great friend's funeral: leaving his home in the South of France he got only as far as the Connaught Hotel and he could go no further – not because he didn't care but because he cared too much. He telephoned me to tell me there was a letter at the porter's desk that was important. I arranged for it to be collected. It was a poem he had written in his room at the Connaught, where he had stayed on his own for several days. It meant then – and still does today – more to me than any other tribute.

For Robin

'At Santa Monica'

'We'll go,' you said,
and walk along
the beach
at Santa Monica.

We'd be, we swore,
English in an
Aliens Land,
and walk barefoot,
with hairy shins,
and trousers rolled
in grey
Pacific sand.

'It's dank!' you said,
'and Dull to boot!'
the Pier
at Santa Monica.

November gulls
swung hard against
an opal sea.
Beer cans bobbed
with plastic cups
and rotting weed.
'No Honey here!' you said,
'for tea.'

But 'Fun!' you said
to be alive and
laugh so much
at Santa Monica.

Hands trailed
London shoes
past musseled rocks
wild blown hair.
Faces winter spumed:
and in my pocket,
(Why just mine?)
all our socks.

'Let's drive!' you said
'barefoot and wet
in Cadillacs'
from Santa Monica.

Left running
Dab-Chicks
fearful of the tide:
polluted molluscs
cups and cans:
and unsuspecting
Benjamins on Carmelina
could not hide!

'Hullo!' you said
'We've come to tea,
quite soaking wet'
from Santa Monica.

Gone now:
Your raven's eye,
the dancing grin,
head held high
and soldier's
unastonished stride.
To write of you
how could I begin?

'We'll go,' you said,
'And walk along the
Beach.
At Santa Monica.'

Index